PRIME MIMICKER

Known to millions for her brilliant
impersonations of Margaret Thatcher,
Barbara Woodhouse, Hilda Ogden and Esther
Rantzen (amongst many others), Janet
Brown has been making people laugh with
the accuracy of her mimicry since – as a child
– she tilted up her nose, stuck out her front
teeth, and in Jessie Matthew's quavery
soprano and incredibly polite English accent
sang, 'Got to donce, Got to Seeng, Got to hev
my leetle fleeng'.

   Her fascinating autobiography covers all
aspects of her life – her childhood near
Glasgow, the early days of serving in a co-op,
her rise to fame, her marriage to popular
comedian the late Peter Butterworth and her
experiences on the journey she made with
the families on the Falkland's Pilgrimage.

   PRIME MIMICKER is a warm and
entertaining story, a marvellous insight into
the personality and career of one of the most
versatile and popular people in show
business today.

Prime Mimicker

Janet Brown

NEW ENGLISH LIBRARY
Hodder and Stoughton

To Tyler and Emma

Copyright © 1986 by Janet Brown

First published in Great Britain in 1986 by Robson Books

New English Library Paperback Edition 1987

British Library C.I.P.

Brown, Janet
  Prime mimicker.
  1. Brown, Janet   2. Entertainers—Great Britain—Biography
  I. Title
  791'.092'4   PN2598.B72/

  ISBN 0 450 41380 2

Printed and bound in Great Britain for Hodder and Stoughton Paperbacks, a division of Hodder and Stoughton Ltd., Mill Road, Dunton Green, Sevenoaks, Kent TN13 2YA.
(Editorial Office: 47 Bedford Square, London WC1B 3DP) by Cox & Wyman Ltd., Reading

Contents

Acknowledgements

Do you mind if I say 'thank you' to one or two people?

To Barbara Nind in the Isle of Wight, who took all my early scribbles and turned them into neat copies. She was also *very persistent* that I keep going.

To Jeremy Robson, who encouraged me so much, and whose patience never fails to surprise me.

And to everyone who has helped put this book together.

I hope for fellow-artistes just starting out it will encourage them if I say that though we have our ups and downs, do hang on – it *can* happen to you.

1

Early Days

ONE DAY, LOOKING THROUGH some press cuttings I'd just received, I read this: 'Janet Brown ran away from home at an early age.' Well, that's nonsense. I would never have dreamed of running away, because I had a very happy home life. Not an exciting one, perhaps, but a very secure and comfortable one – apart from the time when my father was out of work. It puzzled my parents to find me so wrapped up in anything to do with the theatre, but although they would have much rather I'd given up any idea of actually performing, they were loyal and supporting. It's understandable that they should have been concerned about me, for no one in my family had ever had any connection with the theatre.

In 1944, when they sent the 'Stars in Battledress' show to entertain the troops in France, Belgium and Holland, I went with my parents' blessing – even though I wasn't old enough to vote! But that's going forward a long way.

I was born in Scotland, in the Royal Borough of Ruther-glen, just outside Glasgow. 'Ruglonians' were very proud of their borough's royal status, and I can remember a little tongue-twister we used to say:

'Ruglen's wee roon red lums reek briskly.'

Someone in a cabaret room in Australia recently shouted that line out to me when they heard me say that I hailed from Rutherglen, so it's still going strong. Translated, it simply means that Rutherglen's little round red chimneys smoke briskly. It sounds awfully posh put like that, doesn't it? But then Rutherglen actually was posh – or at least Ruglonians thought so, and they were rightly proud of their great wide main street, lined on either side with beautiful leafy trees, and they were proud too of their Town Hall. It wasn't one of your ordinary town halls – oh no! This one had an almost tower-like look about it, grey and craggy, and it absolutely dominated the town. 'What's the time by the Town Hall clock? Have you *seen* our Town Hall? Have you seen our main street?' Ruglonians would say. It was a very busy, bustling place.

I knew the main street well, for I was brought up to be able to shop for my mother. 'Run round to Lipton's and get me some fresh butter, Jenny, and pop in to Aitcheson's for a pound of their home-grown tomatoes.' You always knew the home-grown ones – 'Just pinch the little leaf; it has a special smell.'

As a child, I loved it all, but as I grew older I had other ideas and my father was very upset when one day, sitting having tea at the kitchen table, I burst out that I didn't want to end up leaving school, getting married, then pushing a pram up and down the main street. It was not for me. 'Oh Jenny,' he exclaimed, 'I never thought I'd hear you say a thing like that.'

I can still recall walking down that main street, passing women chatting to each other, standing there in their warm tweed coats, scarves wrapped firmly round their necks to keep out the cold. There always seemed to be time for a chat and as I passed I would hear, just like the sighing of the wind, 'Hoo're y' the day?' 'Oh, no so well.' 'Hoo's yer back?' 'Oh, jist as bad. The doctor says there's no betterness.' Question and answer, moan, moan; it made me laugh and I usually tried to keep those lines in my head so that I could recount them when I got back home again.

I was trying to explain to Russell Harty, when I was a guest on his show, the difference between Glasgow and Rutherglen. I told him that when people hung out of the windows in Rutherglen to have a chat, they always put a cushion on the window ledge where they could rest their elbows. People in Glasgow didn't do that, but they did in Rutherglen! When I met up with the Scottish comedian Andy Cameron, who comes from there, he immediately knew what I was on about. 'Not only was there a cushion on the window ledge,' he told

me, ' but if your Granny thought you were going to lean "oot
the windy" she used to make you wash your face and put your
cap on!'

To get into Glasgow, you took the number 64 bus to
Waterloo Street. The times I queued for that bus! I preferred
buses to trams because I used to be sick on the trams, they
swayed about so much. But gradually I grew out of that and
then I enjoyed running up the winding stairs at the front or the
back, where there was a little nook. Since all the old men with
their evil-smelling pipes puffing great clouds of smoke always
sat upstairs, the nook area, which was open to the elements,
was a better place in which to sit. It was quite a feat to reach
the front without falling into people's laps on the way – the
tram seemed to go at such a fearsome speed. It seems strange
now to hear of a tram being a museum piece, and I think to
myself, 'Good lord, I used to ride on them.'

On Saturday mornings my mother would give me my
instructions. 'Take the tram to the Candleriggs. Get off at
such and such a stop, walk up the left-hand side of the street to
the butcher's shop . . .' All this on your own. I suppose I must
have been around ten or eleven at the time. She did it to instill
a feeling of independence in us; nevertheless it was terrifying.
You were frightened you might get lost, stand at the wrong
tram stop, take the wrong tram home, and Glasgow was such a
busy place on a Saturday. The trams were packed, and
conductresses would lean off their platforms, arms outstretched – 'Come on, get aff!' they'd shout as they helped some on
and pushed others off. It's a contradictory phrase, but a
typically Glasgow one. The poor conductress was driven
frantic trying to keep control of her passengers while at the
same time fishing for change in the heavy leather bag slung
over her shoulder. I recall, too, the clicking of her ticket
machine as she turned her little wheel and handed you a piece
of paper that seemed to come from an endless miniature toilet
roll. We were always taught to give up our seats on buses or
trams to elderly people: it seems strange to me when I read in
the tubes now 'Please vacate the seat for anyone disabled'. It
was just a part of our upbringing to do that automatically.

When you went shopping you took your 'line' with you – this was simply a piece of paper with a list of everything you had to buy. You would go into a shop, hand the 'line' over and the assistant would collect all the things, ticking them off as he placed them on the counter. He would write down the prices, and you would stand there reading his writing upside-down and adding up as fast as you could to try and get the total before he did. I still try and do that. If someone takes out a calculator I want to beat it!

My family (that was my father and mother, my elder brother Bill, younger sister Chris, and myself) lived up what is known in Scotland as a 'close'. This is a corridor-type entry to a tenement building (I'm beginning to feel like a foreigner with all these explanations), and there are still plenty of them around. But there are closes and closes, and ours at number 26 Hamilton Road was one of the better ones. We had green and white tiled walls, unlike the dull brown-painted walls which were always scrawled over with 'messages' – precisely what they said had better not be gone into!

When you entered the close you had to climb three flights of stone stairs to the top floor where we lived. On the first landing a door opened to the back garden, though then we just spoke about 'round the back'. It was only when I had children of my own that I began to appreciate how my mother had to climb up and down those stairs with a pram every time she wanted to go out when we were small. But she thought it worthwhile, all that stomping, step-by-step-by-step, to be out in the street doing her shopping, meeting people and talking to them. She came to see me after I was married and living in the country and said, 'This is no life here, I can't see a familiar face.' At home she knew everyone.

Our home was a small flat, though we always called it a house, with a kitchen and a little scullery, a parlour and a bedroom, a bathroom and a hall – which we called the lobby. How did we all fit in? Well, the kitchen had an alcove containing a double bed, and my father and mother slept there. The parlour was very special, and my mother would often lock the door and hide the key so that the room would stay tidy for visitors; but this room too had an alcove, curtained off, and Bill slept in there. Chris and I slept in the bedroom.

The house had hot and cold running water, the hot water being supplied from the kitchen fire. And there was electric light – I can remember the excitement when that was put in, and the lovely 'click' the switch made as it was moved up or down to on or off. I vaguely remember that before that there was gas – with those fragile little mantles giving out a pale yellow light – but after we'd got electricity it was drummed into us never to leave lights on by mistake. If one of us went into the lobby to get something from the press (that was a big built-in cupboard) we'd make sure to turn the light off as soon as we'd finished. We had an aunt Lizzie, a wonderful character with iron-grey hair that stood up on end, just like Ken Dodd's, who whenever she came to see us used to call out from the kitchen, 'Toot toot, the light!' It's funny how these things stay with you. I still go round switching lights off everywhere!

All our meals were made on the coal-fired range in the kitchen that also heated the water. This range had to be black-leaded – it had an open fire, with an oven door to the left-hand side, and a great flat top where pots and pans went. Above it was a rack where clothes and towels could be kept warm. When years later I visited an aunt of my husband's in Manchester I saw that she had one just like it, but it wasn't the towels warming there, it was the cat. When you think of what facilities there are for cooking now, it was remarkable the meals my mother produced on that stove. There was a little flue thing – I think it was called the damper – and this was opened or closed according to how fast you wanted the fire to burn. In front of the fire was a shiny little steel shelf – oh, the joy at birthday times when my favourite suet dumpling was placed there to cool off. It would sit, currants and raisins popping from its shining skin and the steam rising from it. No one could make a suet dumpling like my mother.

Making up the fire in the morning was quite a ritual. My mother was so thrifty. She plaited newspapers into little rings, like doughnuts, and used these to light the fire. Of course you could buy bundles of sticks, or else chop up boxes, but newspapers were usually handy. Any orange peel would be dried, because it starts a fire beautifully – we learned to use whatever cost least.

The coal was carried up by the coalman – that was a great procedure! There would be a shout and you'd look out of the window down into the street below to see if the coal cart was on its way. When you saw it the big front doors had to be opened up to let the man through. Newspapers had to be put down and things put away because of the dust. The coalman would come staggering through the lobby into the kitchen, bent double with the weight of the bag, and empty the sack into the bunker. This was done to the accompaniment of such advice from my mother as 'Be careful how you do it, mind the dust – put it in gently.' I bet *he* was saying something else under his breath! And no wonder. We might have ordered three bags – just think of it, three times up and down three flights of stairs.

Looking back, I realize just how hard my mother had to work, black-leading the stove and providing us with nourishing meals three times a day. Later on she got a small electric cooker, but for a long time the range in the kitchen was all she had to cook on. And she took, as all Scottish hosewives do, great pride in presenting a well-laid table. It was very important to her when relations came that the white damask cloth was put on, then out would come the best china that was kept in the sideboard in the parlour and the best cutlery from the drawer lined with green baize. There were silver dishes, too, though they were generally kept for New Year. These were in the shape of a basket with a handle, and usually held the New Year bun. Many of these treasures came from her own home, and she liked to place them on the table to make it look really nice. My special job was always to polish up the long silver fork which lay alongside the crystal jar for the beetroot.

The scullery leading off from the kitchen was where the everyday dishes were kept. It was very small – you stepped in

and directly before you was the sink, to the left was where the
dishes were kept and to the right was another area which held
the bread-bin and breadboard. Washing was done in the
scullery sink or in the bathroom – there was no washing
machine, just a green glass scrubbing board. Clothes had to be
put to soak in cold water in the bath, and some of them, such
as my father's overalls, would be filthy. Our spin-dryer then
was a wringer placed across the bath. The clothes would be
put through this before going up on the pulley in the kitchen
or the bathroom. A large handle hung from the side of the
wringer, and woe betide you if you dashed into the bathroom
and bumped into it. You carried the mark for days! But if the
days were brighter we took things down into the back garden.
I was taught the right way to hang a shirt, and put socks up –
'Always peg the toe, Jenny.' On hot days we spread the white
clothes out flat on the grass, and many a time my mother
called from the kitchen window, telling me to throw the
'sapple' – that's the rinsing water – over them to bleach them
in the sun.

There was no such thing as central heating, and the
bedroom in winter was freezing. Chris and I shared a big
double bed. The sheets were icy cold, for hot water bottles
weren't encouraged. 'You make your own heat,' my mother
would say. Not as far as I was concerned! I would tuck my
knees up under my chin and lie huddled in misery, waiting for
my 'own heat' to help make it more bearable. Reading in bed
was discouraged too. If she heard a paper rustling, the
bedroom door would suddenly open and she'd ask sternly,
'Have you got a book in there?' If we had, the chances were
we'd receive a sharp whack. However, if we weren't feeling
well, then it was quite a different matter. A fire was lit in the
bedroom fireplace. It was almost worth while being ill, just to
be able to lie in bed at night, in the dark, with the quilt tucked
warmly round you, and the flames making flickering patterns
on the ceiling. If you've never slept in a bedroom with a coal
fire you can't begin to know how lovely it is (though, come to
think of it, I haven't done it since those early days).

My mother was very capable and a great influence on us all,

but it was my father who had the gentle quality, and I liked
him to look after me if I wasn't feeling well. One time I
jumped from some garden railings, caught my foot and fell
with an awful thud to the ground, jarring (or staving, as we
said) my arms very badly. It was extremely painful, and my
father was the only one who could move or touch my arms – he
had such a sensitive way with him.

I often hear people say the summers were always much
warmer years ago, and I do believe that in my childhood they
were. One of my earliest memories is of my father tossing me
up in the air, and my screams of delight as I practically hit the
kitchen ceiling. I must have been very young. And of
sunshine. I only have to close my eyes and I can feel the heat of
the linoleum beneath my bare feet, and see the pattern I came
to know so well from polishing it. From the kitchen windows
we looked up to the Cathkin Hills. If they were very clear, it
was going to rain. And if you couldn't see them, it *was* raining!

We all had our share of things to do around the house.
Sometimes it was the kitchen or bedroom floor that had to be
polished. The bedroom was my own private studio in a way. I
could polish, sing, and have a look at myself in the wardrobe
mirror while I was doing it. I think I spent more time
watching myself singing and making faces than on dusting. I
always seemed to be singing – flying up the stairs to the top
flat, the air was filled with sound. There was a marvellous
echo, and I loved to hear myself. I don't know if the
neighbours enjoyed it as much as I did – but they certainly
knew when I was about.

Every Friday my job was to wash down the stairs from our
flat. The whiter your steps were the better, so we used a
special cakey-looking white powder in the water. The cloth
was wrung out, then wiped all over the step which would dry
beautifully white. Cleaning brasses was another of my chores;
this included the door handle on the big door, the brass step
and letterbox. Other days I had to take the carpets 'round the
back' and beat them. I really enjoyed knocking hell out of
them and seeing the dust fly up. I get a funny feeling as I write
this that Chris, my sister, got away with quite a lot. She always

seemed to be out playing. My brother Bill wasn't expected to do any housework – that wasn't a man's work. I knew lots of families where the women cleaned the men's shoes, but my father used to do everybody's on a Sunday morning. And I'm almost sure he used banana skins to shine up the brown ones.

My upbringing, and that of my brother and sister too, was a plain one and I've always been very grateful for it. I'm sure it has a lot to do with the steady way I can look at things in the theatrical world I now move in. But it wasn't a dull or a joyless life – my mother had a particularly bright way with her. She would play the piano in the parlour to wake us up in the morning before we went to school, and she took great pleasure in showing us how a Schottische should be done, picking up her skirts and la-la-ing the tune as she danced across the kitchen floor. Harmonizing was another thing she enjoyed. On would go the radio, and if Mother knew the music you could be sure her voice would accompany it. She had lots of odd expressions and ways of looking at things. My husband Pete once asked her what was one of her favourite things, and she replied, 'There's nothing nicer than seeing your washing hanging on the line, and hearing your knickers crack in the wind.' He must have wondered what he was letting himself in for in marrying me!

My mother's Scottish pride showed itself in making sure the house was shining to welcome any visitor, and her prompt payment of bills – I have a vivid picture of her going round to the Co-op, checking there weren't any outstanding debts. She had to be very careful with money, particularly during the years when my father was out of work. She didn't discuss it with me at the time, I was far too young, but later on she told me about having had to make ends meet on very little. I can still see her opening up a packet of tea or sugar and shaking it so well that not a leaf or grain was caught in the wrapping. She told me about the means test, which was such a humiliating experience. It meant that outsiders wanted to know exactly what you had, and for Mother, with her tremendous pride, this stripping away of privacy must have been terrible. But we never went short of food. It was plain, but good. Bowls of home-made Scotch broth full of barley and peas, and at teatime one of my favourite dishes, French toast – fingers of bread dipped in egg, fried in butter and scattered all over with sugar... Delicious! I still have in my kitchen the wooden utensil she used for mashing the potatoes, and I still have the spurtle – that's a straight wooden stick for stirring the porridge.

During the hard time my father was unemployed, we didn't have many holidays – just the odd day away or perhaps a sail down the Clyde. On one memorable outing my mother somehow managed to get the whole family down the gangway and off the boat with only one ticket for the lot of us. She must have had a nerve! And on another less successful one when we were with one of her friends and her family, we all got into a first-class compartment and were promptly turned out by the guard when, on presenting her third-class ticket, my mother said we were just trying out the seats!

My father was a sheet iron worker in Fairfield's shipyard in Govan. He was, I still think, the most gentle man I have ever known, honest and caring, and full of kindness and considera-tion. I loved him very much. Early photographs show a slightly-built man with soft dark brown eyes and receding curly hair, but I remember him as practically bald. My father had a continual battle with work that was really much too heavy for him, but in his quiet way he was proud of his skills, and sometimes, after tea, he would sit trying to work out a problem using marked pieces of cardboard and his set square which he took from a velvet-lined case. This geometry set was very precious, and we all knew better than to play with it.

He once told me that he had wanted to work in a solicitor's office, but instead he had followed in the footsteps of all his brothers. Yet he was different from them. I can remember him talking to me of the pleasures of Milton's *Paradise Lost*, and I recall his delight when I gave him *The Corn is Green* for Christmas, and the enjoyment he got from Emlyn Williams' story of a bright working-class boy who was helped by a strong-minded schoolmistress to break away from the drudgery and poverty of a life of hard manual labour. I think he would have loved to have had the opportunity to read more, to go into another line of work altogether – he knew there was such a lot to read and to learn – but he had to look after us. As a man, it was his responsibility to be the breadwinner for the family; my mother used what he earned, and together they made it go as far as possible. He used to repair our shoes – he had a last – and he would place the shoe on this, then the leather on the sole, and cut carefully round with a big, sharp knife until it was the right shape. Then tacks were hammered in. All this he did after his working hours to save money.

As a little girl I would stand at the parlour window waiting for him to come back from work, watching for the moment when he would come round the corner. He had a long day, for all his working life he rose every morning before six o'clock to travel by tram to the shipyard, right over the other side of Glasgow, carrying the sandwiches my mother had made for him. It sounds odd, I know, but his favourite was a sandwich of little slices of Fry's Chocolate Cream between brown bread. He had his main meal when he got home at night: the Scottish high tea which is a high point in the day. When I go back even now, it's almost a source of offence not to have that tea, though it can be tough if you've eaten a big lunch (not that Dad would have had anything hot since his boiled egg or whatever for breakfast). But in Scotland 'Come for your tea' usually means that pancakes, ginger cakes, wheaten scones, plain scones and cream cakes will all be sitting there waiting to welcome you. It's a Scottish way of saying how pleased they are to see you.

I remember, too, how upset my father was when, like so many others in the 1930s, he became unemployed – a feeling of disgrace at not having a job. As far as I can recall he was out of work for about three years, but it's possible that it wasn't quite so long. It was so awful for him to have to make excuses to people – I know he felt that they might think he wasn't looking for a job, or didn't want to work, whereas in fact he tried desperately to take anything that came along. But there were so few jobs around. Eventually, my Aunt Mary, Dad's sister, helped him get a job in the paper factory in Lairds

where she worked, but this was even heavier work than he'd
been accustomed to in the shipyard and he ended up in
hospital. I have a memory of him on his return -- standing at
the door looking terribly tidied up instead of in his overalls,
and wearing one of those strange bowler hats.

Dad's favourite pastimes were football in the winter, and
bowls in the summer. He took me with him later on to several
football matches, and we stood on the terraces while the
remarks shouted at the referee and players sailed round my
ears: 'Heh, you, kick the ball! Go on, kick it! Aw Jeeze, would
you look at that! Away and bile yer heed!' I loved it all. And it
has certainly left its mark on me. It's no uncommon thing for
my children to hear me shriek and shout when a match is on
television.

During the football season his brothers – my Uncle Joe,
Uncle Jim and Uncle Willie – would come out to the house
after the match. Mother just knew there'd be a ring at the bell,
and there they'd be: tall, rain-coated, capped and ready for
their tea. On those Saturday afternoons the table would be
loaded down with good things. We would all sit round eating
our steak pie – a great Scottish favourite – or one of my
mother's fish dishes such as sole rolled up, covered with
beaten eggs and baked in a casserole in the oven. Then the
discussion would take place. Every move of the game would
be gone over again, and great was the gloom if their team had
lost. Dad filled in the Pools all his life, but I don't recollect any
grand wins.

Sunday was very much the Sabbath day. You didn't go out
and play, and – believe it or not – people even pulled their
blinds down. We all went obediently to church, wearing our
Sunday best. My mother had a great thing about Dad looking
good. When he was all ready in his best suit and his soft brown
hat, she'd say, 'Put on your leather gloves, Andrew, you'll
find them in the hallstand.' And Dad's reply was always the
same: 'I'll carry them, Nellie.' He just didn't feel at ease with
them on.

My sister Chris and I were often dressed alike and I
remember one particular outfit my mother made – Donegal

tweed coats and hats to match. She was such a good
seamstress.

The walk down the main street to Munro Church, which
was Church of Scotland, was a long one, and to the reminders
to 'walk properly and not dirty your white socks' we would
finally arrive at the big doors just as the bells stopped chiming
for the eleven o'clock service. We had a pew of our own in
what was called the 'dooket' or dove-cote -- an area apart from
the main body of the church where you were not so easily
seen. However, when you spotted the odd boy you'd taken a
fancy to, then you leaned forward hoping you could be seen
from his side of the balcony! The seats were hard and wooden,
and the pew had a little wooden door that closed. Church-
going of this sort was no pleasure to me. I simply did it
because it was expected. The minister would hold forth – and
they did hold forth a lot – so that you never knew how long the
sermon was going to last. It was really heavy going. They had
very strong views on many subjects and as I grew older I felt I
couldn't join the church, because I didn't agree with what they
were saying. I knew the general procedure was to become a
member, and take on responsibilities. It was a very big step.
Inwardly, as I listened, I said, 'I can't do that.' As a child on
those heavy Sabbath mornings I passed the time making a
handkerchief mouse jump up my arm, or if the minister's
voice was still droning on I'd say under my breath this little
verse:

> *This is the church*
> *This is the steeple,*
> *Open the door*
> *And there's the people.*

After the long morning service, when I'm sure lots of
women at any rate were hoping to be out in time to get the
soup on and the dinner started, we were still not finished with
church. There was another church at the end of Hamilton
Road, and we went to Sunday School there in the afternoon.

It was also there that I became a member of the teetotal
Band of Hope. We had banners and we sang hymns with great

gusto and I signed the temperance pledge. A great event was the church soirée. The hall was always packed, everyone knew everyone. It was a great atmosphere.

'Sit next to me, Annie.'

'Come on, you move up, Jimmy.'

The lights would go down, and all the shuffling and laughing would stop. A hush would fall over the audience, and the entertainment begin. Songs, sketches, recitations. I took part in one concert, standing on the stage in the warmth of the lights, clutching a flower basket and nervously singing the old Victorian ballad of the flower-seller,

'Underneath the gas-light's glitter . . .,' my voice becoming more and more wobbly.

Sunday School trips were the best, outings on the train, and – joy of joys – actually sitting with your friends in a compartment all on your own. No Sunday School teacher in charge. You felt terribly grown up! When we reached our destination there was a hive of activity in the field where the outing was being held. Pegs were hammered into the ground, and tapes went up in preparation for the races. After it all there were big urns of tea and hot pies, and we would all go home thoroughly happy.

I attended dancing classes in the Church Hall and the Sunday School parties wearing little black pumps with a cross of elastic at the ankle, and a pretty pink silk dress. Most of our entertainment was provided either at church or at home. Home was always cheerful, with the fire crackling away and the radio on. I know we listened to Children's Hour, and I remember listening to the Glasgow Orpheus Choir and my sister sticking a bead up her nose! Strains of *Jerusalem* were forgotten as panic set in and everybody tried to get it down. I was told to run round to Penman's, the newsagents', and buy some snuff. I think that must have brought it down. If it didn't, she's the only women I know with a bead up her nose!

We didn't have a lot of money, but we had plenty of fun just the same. Dad had a great way of telling a story, and I loved to sit at the table while he was having his tea and hear him relate some funny tale about what had happened that day in the shipyard.

Hallowe'en was always a time when we all let our hair down, playing all kinds of games. There was one I especially liked – trying to take a bite out of a scone covered in black treacle. What made it difficult was that it was tied on to the end of a piece of string that hung from the pulley in the kitchen. The more you tried to take a bite, the more the scone swung away. You had to stand on tiptoes to try and reach it. What a mess it made, but the laughs were great! Ducking for apples was another hilarious activity, leaning over the back of a chair with a fork in your mouth and trying to spear a rosy apple from a big bowl below. The bowl was filled with water, and the apples were given a good stir to make them bob about like mad – almost impossible to catch.

I was reminding my brother recently of some of those things, and he said, 'Do you remember how we used to go to the farmer and ask for a turnip?'

'Of course I do,' I said. 'And how we cut eyes and mouth in it before hollowing it out and placing a candle inside.'

It made a frightening face! Then off we would go to the neighbours with the lantern face on a string, to sing a song or to recite. They would give us something to put in the bag we had with us, apples or nuts – or if we were very fortunate, some money. But we always had to perform.

In the evenings my mother knitted a great deal, and either Chris or myself had to sit with arms outstretched, holding a skein of wool which my mother wound into seemingly endless balls for making jerseys or socks for us.

I don't think we expected to be entertained in an elaborate way. When we were very young we painted pictures or read our books, and when we were a bit older, there was homework to be done. But if our grown-up cousins came it was great fun. We would have songs round the piano, and Dad giving us a tune on his mandolin. His other instruments were the Jew's harp and some old bones he called 'clappers'. I'd play his favourite tune on the piano, and he would accompany me, hammering these bones up and down his arms. Not very

musical, but who cared? We were all involved in having a good
time together.

On Saturdays there was the cinema. The noise at the
matinee was really dreadful! Full of children shouting at the
baddies and cheering for the goodies. The films that stick in
my memory are westerns, where the cowboys always seemed
to be finding places in the rocks where the cattle had gone in.
Usually the baddie had hidden them away. Then an aeroplane
would fly across overhead, making a lot of noise so that the
cattle would look up.

New Year's Day was very special, but Christmas was all
excitement and presents. When I was a little girl I used to
hang my knickers from the mantelpiece with drawing pins,
using big safety pins to secure the legs so that the brown paper
parcels couldn't fall through! Somehow brown paper parcels
are always much more exciting, I think, than ones done up in
coloured Christmas wrapping.

New Year was quite different. My father always came to us
in the bedroom and wakened Chris and myself up. 'A Happy
New Year,' he'd say, then give both of us a kiss and hand us a
glass of ginger wine. He'd bring us the silver basket full of
shortbread and New Year bun – a very heavy bun, thick with
fruit, which Mother made and which we all had to stir before
it went into the oven. It didn't have an iced top, was just left
plain, and to be quite honest I didn't really like it. It was much
too rich for me and I usually stuck to the shortbread. That was
lovely, all crumbly and buttery.

It was a day when you visited other relatives, wearing your
very best clothes. And they in turn came to see you.

'Happy New Year,' was all you heard, accompanied by
endless handshaking. We weren't a family that went in for
'first-footing'. Visiting houses after midnight and sharing your
bottle with them was no part of our home life because neither
of my parents drank. But they were always happy to see
visitors on New Year's morning, no matter how early; it was
all part of the fun.

I wasn't the only one in the family who enjoyed standing on a stage – my brother Bill had his moments of glory too. He was a Scout, and always took part in the Gang Shows, usually playing comedy parts. He was very funny. I sometimes wonder if he might have had a secret yearning to do more in this line. However, because we all needed to earn something as soon as possible, he didn't stay on at school, but left and joined the Post Office as a telegram boy. I'm sure he hated it – wearing the heavy navy blue uniform and cycling round Rutherglen in all weathers. But security was a word you heard continually. A secure job meant everything, and I know my father and mother felt that they were doing the best for him at the time. In fact, he stayed with the Post Office all his working life and finally became the Area Telephone Manager at Norwich.

Music has always been part of my life; I had cousins who played the piano and violin, a brother who played the banjo – and there was my mother's harmonizing and even my father's tunes on the mandolin. Chris had a very sweet voice. I visited her not long ago in Canada and she sang for us one night at a party. The notes were as warm and true as ever. It took me back to the times when, in our teens, we used to sit at the piano – me playing Vera Lynn's song 'Yours', and both of us harmonizing together. We thought we were great. I suppose it is natural really that this love of music should tumble into my present family life. In our house tripping over a trombone or bumping into a set of drums is quite an everyday occurrence!

Going back to those early days, I think we were fortunate there were so many relations around us. Visitors stirred me with excitement. I loved seeing the outline of someone through the frosted glass of the front door, and trying to guess who it might be. When I was small I always found it difficult to get to sleep later on if I could still hear the sound of talk and laughter coming from the kitchen. A knock at the door or the bell jangling had you running to find out who had come to visit you. Often it was Aunt Mary – no sooner was she in the lobby than she'd say: 'Now let's see what I can find in my handbag. ...' Oh, the anticipation as she delved into the

bottom of her large leather bag, sometimes coming up with
toffee, other times with 'tablet' that she had bought at the
church bazaar. 'Tablet' is home-made fudge that melts in your
mouth, leaving a most satisfying taste. It was such a treat.
Friends tell me that I make a glass of water sound like a treat –
if that's true, it's because as a child everything *was* to me a
special treat.

Aunt Mary and Aunt Kate were my father's sisters, and
they often came out to our house in Rutherglen. Like my
uncles, they would just arrive – but never together; it was
either Aunt Mary, or Aunt Kate. If we were not at home, it
was just too bad. They seemed quite happy, to use their own
expression, to take 'pot luck'. Sometimes they would leave a
note: 'Dear Nellie – called, but you were out.' But most times
we were there, and more than pleased to see them.

Aunt Mary, who worked all her life in Lairds paper factory,
was small in build, and wore thick pebbly horn-rimmed
glasses. One of her jobs was to make little fancy paper bags for
holding pieces of wedding cake. She never made any for my
wedding, but more of that later. Staying with my Aunt Mary
and Aunt Kate in Govan was not something Chris or I
particularly enjoyed. Perhaps it was because they had chairs
with horsehair seats – my word, how they scratched your legs!
On the other hand, the ivory fan pinned to the wall and the
green and white crystal ornaments on the mantelpiece
intrigued me, especially when you made them touch one
another to produce a pretty tinkling sound. Nowadays, it's the
thing to make them into lamp bases.

If Aunt Mary could be moody, she could also be very kind.
I think she was probably the person who first encouraged my
liking for the theatre, and she was the one who saw to it that
we learned to ride a bicycle. She even gave us a bike. I still
remember that wonderful feeling of really pedalling away
(after falling off when I found that nobody was holding the
seat!)

My Aunt Kate was a complete contrast. Neither of these
aunts ever married, but Kate was tall and strikingly elegant.
She wore clothes with great style, even though she didn't have

a lot of money to spend on them, and she had a great liking for lovely dangly ear-rings. They were usually jade, or tortoiseshell, and they absolutely fascinated me, especially when in conversation she turned her head from side to side.

There are two expressions I can't bear. One is 'Wait till you're my age'. The other, 'Of course, people of my generation. . . .' This was Aunt Kate's favourite, and each time I heard her say it I thought to myself, 'When I grow up, I'll *never* use that phrase' – and I never have. Silly really, but I always felt it put people into different categories.

She had another odd expression. When she spoke about the Queen Mother, who then was the Queen, she always referred to her as 'Hail Smiling Morn', perhaps because whatever picture you saw of the Queen, she was always smiling. And if we said, 'Doesn't she look beautiful?', Aunt Kate would reply crisply, 'Oh yes, but fine feathers make fine birds.'

On my mother's side there was Aunt Maggie from Stirling. She lived in a fine terraced house full of beautiful antiques. It was all vastly different from my home and visits to her were quite an occasion. She was a complete contrast to my mother. Mother was hearty and outspoken, Aunt Maggie soft-voiced, and 'very genteel' as they say in Scotland. But if we looked forward to going to *her* house, she certainly felt the same about coming to *ours*. Having no children of her own, I think it gave her great pleasure to feel part of the family. I know she enjoyed sitting in front of the fire having her tea, it was all so warm and friendly. At tea-time I couldn't take my eyes off her. She had a compulsive need to fidget with her hands.

'You know, Nellie, I just thought I'd go and see if Mr Williams was in and have a wee word with him,' her hand nervously smoothing over the tablecloth. 'I said to him, you know, Mr Williams, this won't do at all . . .' By now, the forks and knives had been picked up and put down, spoons straightened in their saucers and plates re-positioned – on and on it went until she had practically re-laid the table! She also had a habit of tracing patterns across the tablecloth with her fork, usually when explaining something in detail, while my mother – listening with great interest – made little designs on the sugar in the bowl with the back of her sugar spoon. I've seen lots of people do that – it's odd how they can't leave the sugar bowl alone. Have you noticed how some people keep pinching little bits of coffee sugar and crunching them up throughout their conversation?

Another of my mother's sisters, Aunt Ella, had a wonderful habit. She used to re-pleat the hem of her dress while she chatted, pinching it together between her finger and thumb and making little pleats till it was almost up round her neck!

As well as all these aunts, we also had cousins, who were quite a bit older than us. Some of my happiest times were on visits to them. Uncle Joe was married to Aunt Sarah – she was a gentle person and spoke with a very soft voice. She wore her hair all piled up in a big bun, and I remember she loved eating peanuts – come to think of it, I did too, and we'd sit together happily cracking away at the shells till the table looked more like a battlefield. They had four children – two sons and two daughters. Sadly, William, one of the sons, was lost at sea when his submarine, the *Thetis*, went down on its trial run.

Uncle Joe and Aunt Sarah lived in between Kilmacolm and Port Glasgow, high on the hill just before you come to Greenock. The bus used to stop outside where they lived with my cousins Chris, May and Jimmy. From the sitting-room window you had a wonderful view of the River Clyde and across to Dunbarton Rock. We could see all the ships as they passed on their way to the Tail of the Bank and then on out to sea.

I have a faint memory of one very exciting day. Everyone in the family seemed to be there, with uncles and aunts galore, and children running in and out of the house, and to crown it all a splendid high tea. What was all the excitement about? Well, it was a party for the launching of the *Queen Mary*. We all waited in the back garden, and as the great ship sailed majestically past, we cheered our heads off.

Chris and May, the sisters, had their own draper's shop at the bottom of Clune Bray. It was small, but packed with everything under the sun. There were boxes of lisle stockings and silk stockings, and boxes of underslips, vests and underskirts, and long pink corsets with dangling silver suspenders nestling in narrow cardboard boxes. There were drawers that held masses of coloured ribbons, drawers bulging with babies' dresses and drawers full of women's aprons.

It was pretty dark in the shop, but the back shop was even darker. This was a small store-room packed with merchandise. You went up a couple of steps and through a curtain, and in there was the teapot and gas ring. If we were sitting behind the curtain and we heard someone come in, we'd run out to serve them. I loved being behind the counter, and the look of surprise on the customer's face. 'Oh, is this your cousin?' they'd ask. Or, 'I see you've got a new helper.' When Chris or May replied, 'Yes, this is my new assistant,' my cup was full. Of course they knew everybody in Port Glasgow, and everybody knew the Brown sisters, for they listened and shared in people's problems. Both had a most sympathetic manner. Chris had a way of saying 'Oh' that covered everything. 'My wee girl's no very well,' someone might tell her. 'Oh,' and the note would go right down. 'She's been ill for three weeks.' 'Oh' – a long sympathetic one. 'But the doctor says she's improving.' 'Oh,' again, but this time full of delight. I was always fascinated by this sound, indeed I still am. Only recently I overheard a Scots woman in front of me on a bus telling another some long drawn-out story, while her friend sat nodding her head and giving a whole range of replies with just 'hmm hmm', 'hmm hmm'. I think it's only in Glasgow you could get a sound like that.

To stay with my cousins was a special treat. They were so kind to both my sister Chris and to me, knowing exactly the kind of things little girls would be thrilled with. If they gave us a handbag they'd finished with, inside it there'd be a little compact of powder and rouge. Sometimes a perfume was found to put in it as well, with the exotic title 'Evening in Paris'. And there was always some money to go and buy sweets next door.

Their brother Jimmy had a small shoe-mending business in Gourock. Like Aunt Sarah he was quiet and gentle and he liked to play the occasional tune on the violin or the piano. I always experienced a nice feeling of pleasure and anticipation every time I stayed at Port Glasgow.

I can't recall my father objecting to our playing with the odds and ends of make-up our cousins gave us when we were little girls. However, when I was older and he saw me put on powder he was quite definite: 'Jenny, you don't need anything like that on your face.' But I enjoyed seeing myself in the mirror looking – as I thought – very sophisticated, particularly when I used liquid rouge. I'd pat this on carefully with a small sponge. I even put it on for one of the first broadcasts I ever did – of course nobody could see it, but I felt very grown-up.

Perhaps my interest in 'beauty' did start young, however; though I'd quite forgotten some of the things I used to do until a *Sunday Express* article on the uses of cucumber jogged my memory. I started to read part of it out to my daughter, Emma:

·'Listen, Emma, doesn't this sound interesting? You can mash up a cucumber, mix it with honey and then apply it as a face mask.'

Her reaction was straightforward. 'Ugh, how awful! What a mess!' And then I found myself telling her how, as a little girl, I had this great horror of wrinkles. I must have been all of nine years old, and I used to beat up an egg white, put it in a saucer, then dab it under my eyes and lie in the bath with a completely rigid face. Another thing I did was to cut out small squares of muslin, fill them with fine oatmeal and then tie them tightly – the idea being that the oatmeal would soften the water, but more often than not the basin was filled with grains of oatmeal. Perhaps I didn't tie the muslin tightly enough?

But my *pièce de résistance* was the pig's trotter! I tied that to the bath tap and rubbed my hands with it to keep them smooth! Goodness knows what my mother thought of all this – she had a marvellous skin, and used nothing but soap and water all her life.

Of course, my ideas of what was beautiful were not always the same. When I started school, I longed to have a face that shone like a polished apple – like that of my friend May Watson. I used to rub at it with a towel, until it was quite sore, but I could never achieve her round rosy gleaming look. She was a very capable little girl – she could take a newspaper and cut it out to make a dress pattern, then put that on the material and make up a garment. I was defeated by this. We both attended the Gallowflat Primary School, and while we were there I tried to make a pair of knickers. After inspecting them the teacher made the cutting remark: 'There's room for two pillows and bolster in there!' I was left-handed, and this presented terrible problems, especially later on when I worked in the Co-op. For a while I served in the fabric department. Unrolling a bale of material, measuring it out and finally cutting it filled me with dread, and many a time the customer found a pair of scissors being handed over with the plea: 'Can you cut it from your side, please?'

It was while I was at Gallowflat School that I sang in my first concert. I was probably four-and-a-half to five, and I think I wore a little crocheted dress in pale pink or blue. My part in the concert was to stand in a circle of children and sing a verse or chorus on my own. I can't remember the song, but I do remember the warmth of the spotlight, and the thrill of the applause – it's a feeling that stayed with me when I eventually went in for talent competitions, and I experience it even now.

I started school very early, but the Gallowflat School was only just along the road – and I was very keen to be there. My memories – apart from the concert – are of a great big classroom divided by folding doors, with large pictures of Bible stories round the walls. And sand trays to draw in. . . . I stayed until I was eleven, before passing my exams for the Rutherglen Academy. For the most part I think I behaved myself, but occasionally I did something to anger the teacher. My punishment, as it was a mixed school, was to be moved over to sit with the boys. It was a nice punishment, I thought!

One of my teachers, Miss Thompson, had a wonderful way of telling a story. Watching her, as she opened her desk and brought the book out, was just the start. Then she would place it in front of her, open it very carefully and press her hand firmly against the pages to flatten them. That movement, and the slight pause before she began, always filled me with expectancy – what story were we going to hear today? The class waited, hushed.

She had a very quick temper, and if someone wasn't paying attention, or was doing something wrong, a rolled-up belt, or the strap as we called it, would come flying across the room. She had an excellent aim, and you had to duck out of the way pretty smartly! If anyone really misbehaved, they were called out in front of the class and told to hold their hand out. The strap had thongs on the end, and when Miss Thompson brought it down on your outstretched hand you certainly knew it – it smarted so badly. Some of my schoolfriends were terribly nervous and found it impossible not to flinch and draw their hands away, but it made no difference – they still had to face up to the punishment.

We held concerts at the end of term, going round all the classrooms with sketches and songs. Fancy dresses were made out of crêpe paper, or you found something from home if you were playing a character.

I was happy at school, even though – as I'll explain in the next chapter – I wasn't there very long. I had lots of friends, both at Gallowflat and later on, after I'd passed the eleven-plus, at the Rutherglen Academy. I liked English, but was hopeless at maths, which I hated; in fact I wasn't an academic type at all. Neither was I sporty – I never wanted to run around madly, hitting a ball and being part of a hockey team or anything like that. I played a little tennis, but I really wasn't very good. During a game with my sister once, she said angrily: 'This is no good, I want to play with someone who'll improve my game.' I think that says it all.

Looking back, I realize Gallowflat was a good school. It seemed enormous to me then, with its separate cookery block for the girls and woodwork rooms for the boys. Morning assembly was quite a production – we marched out of the hall and up the stairs, then along the balconies – one-two, one-two, keeping time while one of the teachers played the piano, until, rather like the children in *The Pied Piper of Hamelin*, we disappeared into our respective classrooms.

It makes me laugh now to think of the playground and

playtimes. Playtime! Small children sitting with their backs
against the wall like a lot of little old ladies, crocheting away at
scarves and hats for their dolls, the crochet needle laboriously
moving in and out of the squares – can you imagine it? I don't
think I'd know one end of a crochet hook from the other now.
The games we played were the kind that got the circulation
going. There was one called 'Barley sugar'. You and your
partner stood at arms' length, grasped each others' hands
firmly and away you went, each pulling the other, whirling
like a windmill round the playground – the faster and more
furious it became, the hotter your cheeks. When this game
was over I used to have to go and run my wrists under cold
water to cool me down. With your heart pounding and your
face scarlet you thought you were going to collapse.

I suppose playtimes will always follow a pattern, and
children will always play the games I used to play – doing
handstands where you throw your legs up against a wall, and
your skirts fall down over your head showing your knickers.
And leapfrog, and cartwheels. . . .

At the Academy, where I spent little more than two years,
we were taught Latin and French, and attended Science
classes with gas jets and Bunsen burners, and mysterious
liquids bubbling away. We wore navy-blue gymslips, and I
think a blue and yellow Academy tie. I remember walking to
school on boiling hot days, and the pleasure of bursting all the
tar bubbles on the road. I still love the smell of tar.

It was while I was there that I entered a singing competition
at one of the churches. As usual I was shaking with nerves.
When I finished, the adjudicator remarked that my singing
was 'like sliding up and down a greasy pole'. If I had a
character to hide behind, I didn't shake – a character
presented no problems, but singing was another matter. To
stand in front of the class and sing, just being myself, was a
nightmare. Reciting was easy, and I won prizes for that. One
of my favourite pieces, I remember, was called 'The Next
Stop's Kirkcaldy' – this was a poem about a little boy's long
train journey. So you see, hiding behind a character is how the
impressions started, but I'll go on to that later.

People sometimes say to me that it must take great nerve to stand up and face an audience, but I don't think of it that way. It may seem strange, but I could never have marched down Rutherglen main street as a member of the Girl Guides – the fear of not doing it correctly, and the thought of people who knew me watching and, horror of horrors, perhaps being the only one out of step – no, to me that really took nerve. Somehow, on a stage entertaining an audience it's completely different. It might sound ridiculous, but you don't know anybody personally and so you don't feel self-conscious. You're working to an area, to a feeling, establishing a rapport between yourself and the audience. Now, of course, if I'm working in cabaret, I love seeing people's faces around me and making contact – but back in those early days I was just terribly nervous, and shook and shook.

I'd quite forgotten that people do shake like that, but while on a cruise I was invited to a Masonic function on board the ship. The Lodgemaster made a speech, and his glass shook so badly that he had to pass it to someone else to hold while he said his few lines of welcome. I felt really sorry for him. One of my party was convinced that he had Parkinson's Disease! But later on that night we were all enjoying some entertainment, and there was the self-same Lodgemaster drinking away happily and holding his glass as steady as a rock, not a shake in sight. There was absolutely nothing wrong with him, and I thought 'You poor man – I know the feeling. I've done that!'

2

I've Made A Start!

My earliest memory of what theatre is all about goes back to when I was around five or six. My parents had taken me to see a summer show in Gourock – someone must have asked children to come up on the stage, because I do remember standing in the company of the other artistes. There was a singing act then called the Troy Sisters and Sidney Wilson, and they took me to their dressing-room. That was the first time I'd ever been in one. One of the sisters was about to play a nurse in a sketch, and after I'd watched her put on a white overall she took a white paper bag, folded it carefully into a strip and attached it to her head with two hairclips. This 'nurse's cap' was the first theatre prop I ever saw.

But Christmas was the time of year when we were taken into Glasgow to see a pantomime – what a wonderful, exciting word, and what a wonderful exciting feeling as you made your way to your seats. The best were in the front of the circle.

'Open the chocolates before it starts, Jenny.' Cellophane wrappers made such a noise. Then a whispered 'Pass them along,' as the overture began.

Here we go! The curtain rising to reveal the stage, a blaze of colour – girls and boys dancing round a maypole, their faces looking very bright with make-up. But my favourite moments were the scenes with the trap-door, and the demon king, and the dames suddenly appearing or disappearing.

Glasgow was a great city for pantomime, and you had a fine choice of theatres. The King's, the Theatre Royal, the Alhambra, the Pavilion, the Metropole, and the Empress. As a child I saw many famous comedians – Will Fyfe, and George Lacey as dame – I can still see him with a tight black velvet dress on his long slim figure – a sequined question mark on his back. This raised a great laugh from the audience when he turned up-stage. There were others I grew up with, like Tommy Morgan, whose accent was so broad I never knew what he was saying. He had a way of blowing his cheeks out and making them quiver, then saying his catch-phrase 'Clairty-clairty' – I still don't know what it means, but again the audience laughed. All the Scottish comedians had catch-phrases. Perhaps the most well-known of these was 'It's away up a ky' – that was Dave Willis's. With his little black bowler hat and moustache, everybody loved him and his sketches were hilarious. It's a curious thing, I had to learn to 'project' in the theatre, yet Dave could stand there and talk, and you could hear every word. By the way, if you're wondering what 'way up a ky' means, I think it's when a small child saw an aeroplane in the sky and trying to describe it, said 'It's away up a'ky.'

Looking back now, I realize I owe a lot to my Aunt Mary. She encouraged my love of the theatre. Often when she visited us to take 'pot-luck' as usual, she said, 'The Wilson Barrett Company are presenting such and such a play tonight. Would you like to see it?' Would I! In no time we were off in the bus to Glasgow. They were an immensely popular repertory company, and Aunt Mary was one of their greatest fans.

It was the amphitheatre we made for with its endless stairs, and once we'd climbed them all, there'd be a great scurrying and scrambling for the best positions in the front row. There were no separate seats, just long wooden benches, and we were terribly, terribly high up! I used to look over the rail and far below I'd see the stage and watch the audience coming into the stalls – I often wondered if I'd ever sit down there in the expensive seats. I can't be certain that I had thoughts of actually standing on a stage then, but I do know that I loved being inside the theatre. The lights would go down and we'd sit for a moment in the darkness. A hush would fall over the audience just before the curtain rose – you could feel the anticipation as it began to go up, and then – there was the play!

You have to get tuned into dialogue when a play first starts, and high up in the amphitheatre there was certainly quite a bit of tuning in to be done. But this kind of thing works both ways. I always felt that extra contact with the artistes when they looked up to the gods – a kind of reaching out that made you feel so good because, high up as you were, you were still included. I think of that now when I'm working in a theatre. The late Maurice Fournier, one of Bernard Delfont's top directors, once made a remark that has proved valuable to me: 'The artistes who have been playing clubs a lot always give themselves away, you only see the tops of their heads because they work only to the people around them and never look up.'

How can you get started in the theatre? This is a question I'm often asked, and I don't think there's any one way. For me it began with talent contests – but long before that, because the desire must have been very deep in me, I found ways to learn more. I can play the piano by ear, but when I was quite a little girl I went to the library and found a children's encyclopaedia with instructions on how to play it properly, and how to read music. Black notes were gnomes and white notes fairies!

My parents gave me a ukelele to practise a George Formby impression, for he was one of the most popular stars. I patiently worked out the fingering on the frets from sheet music and song books. Joining the local choir to learn harmonies was also a help. Have you ever sung in harmony? It's a wonderful feeling to hear other voices blending with yours and I've never forgotten that first experience – me with my soprano tones, next to me the contralto, then tenor and bass. All of us producing the haunting strains of the Londonderry Air: 'Oh Danny Boy, the pipes, the pipes are calling....' It may only have been a simple hall we rehearsed in, but I was completely lifted out of myself, and it gave me a great sense of achievement.

To return to the talent contests. These were held in Glasgow, and usually run by one of the cinemas. I was encouraged to enter them when I was around thirteen by a Mrs Brown (no relation at all) who ran a sweet shop at the end of our road. She had seen me singing and pretending to play the piano along the ledge of the shop window. Mrs Brown had an artistic eye – her sweets were always very attractively arranged, the chocolates displayed in little bowls nestling in amongst folds of pale green crêpe de chine. I'd often collect leaves from the woods and bring them to Mrs Brown to place in between the chocolates. The leaves looked especially nice when they were turning to their rich, reddish autumn colours.

Sometimes I'd help her behind the counter, weighing out a quarter pound of chocolate dates (one of my favourites) and then sliding them off the little shiny brass scale pan into a paper bag. A day spent at Mrs Brown's house was fun. She played the piano very well, and would accompany me while I happily sang my songs. All over the avenue you could hear the notes of 'Is it true what they say about Dixie?' The song took a terrible hammering, and so did the neighbours who had to listen to it!

If I owed a lot to my Aunt Mary, I certainly owed a great deal to Mrs Brown. She loved everything to do with the theatre, and revelled in taking me into Glasgow to the auditions and competitions. It was she who really got me started. In a way it was rather like having an agent or a manager, though I knew nothing about such things then.

My parents never minded Mrs Brown taking me to all the auditions – in fact all the Browns were very good friends. There were other friends' houses I used to visit as well – possibly they were intrigued by this little girl who liked to sing and play different characters. Among these friends were Jack and Betty Stewart: Jack owned a radio shop in Great Western Road, and occasionally did football commentaries for the BBC. He even rigged up a mike in the sitting room – I had the time of my life singing into it and pretending I was famous.

The talent contests in the Glasgow cinemas were tremendously popular. They were generally put on between the two feature films. Each person was given a few minutes to do their act. At the end everyone trooped back on stage again, this time for the compere to ask the audience which of us was to be the lucky winner.

One of the first impressions I ever did was of Jessie Matthews. You may have known her better as Mrs Dale in the radio series 'Mrs Dale's Diary', but I first saw her in a musical at the Alhambra Theatre. I watched her through opera glasses, for as usual we were very high up, and oh! how fragile she looked, wearing one of those glamorous chiffon dresses that flowed and swirled around her as she danced. Her dancing was beautifully graceful, and there was this amazing kick that she did – touching the side of her head with her foot. But the voice was the thing – terribly wobbly, and to my Scottish ears unbelievably polite. Each phrase was enunciated very carefully. I bought a copy of one of these songs, 'Got to dance, got to sing'. Her picture was on the front of it. She had enormous dark brown eyes that looked out from under a deep fringe, a turned-up nose and protruding teeth. I learned the number and bought her record, playing and re-playing it as she sang:

> Got to donce,
> Got to seeng,
> Got to have my leetle fleeng.
> Got to donce my way to heaven
> Right in your orms ...

I kept practising it over and over until I finally felt it was right.

There is always something that draws you particularly to a character, and for me it was her voice, then the teeth. So I put my finger under my nose to tilt it, stuck my teeth out, and away I went – singing as best I could the Jessie Matthews way. It was the kind of thing audiences liked, and they laughed a lot.

Other impressions I did then were Mae West and Shirley Temple. My mother made all my dresses, including a Shirley Temple one that was covered with a gingham dress with large poppers – I could just rip it off to show the other underneath. Shirley Temple had a little round mouth with dimples on each side and when she sang 'On the Good Ship Lollipop' she held up one finger. I made sure I did this too. The word 'scriptwriter' was no part of my vocabulary – I'd never heard of them – and so I took jokes from the papers and strung them together. I can't remember the first lines I used for Mae West, but I know it was something to do with being celestial, 'Because I've got a heavenly body'. She always spoke in a kind of chewing-gum way, rolling the words round in her mouth, touching her hair and smoothing her hips. No other actress has ever waggled her hips like Mae West. I loved doing her.

It's funny little incidents that stick in your mind. I remember going to an audition where everyone had to wait in an ante-room. I noticed they all kept drinking glasses of water. I'd no idea why they were doing it, but I thought I'd better do the same – I know now it means your throat is dry from nerves but at that time I didn't know about that either! Suddenly I heard my name and I was out on a big black stage with a spotlight blinding my eyes. I was unable to see anything but darkness. It gave me the strange feeling of just looking into space – no people. (I've had that feeling since – but usually first house in a summer show!) At the end, there was the usual line-up: the compere holding his hands above the head of each contestant in turn and listening to the applause, then choosing the finalists. I was one of them – the others were a group of singers who had sung – for some unknown reason, since after all it *was* Scotland – 'Men of Harlech'. Great excitement! We were asked to return on another night to repeat our act for the audience. This time the winner was chosen.

'Ladies and gentlemen, the winner is—' and I heard them give the name of the singers. They were handed a big silver cup – I'm sure it couldn't really have been silver, it must have been silver-plated – and I was given the second prize of £5. £5! It was a fortune, and the singers obviously felt I'd got the best of the bargain. I dashed home, hardly able to wait to show Dad and Mother what I'd won, ran up the stairs, flew into the kitchen, said 'Look at this!' and threw my five single pound notes up in the air. They were delighted.

When I was about 13 I won one of these talent shows, and the organizer suggested that I should join a touring stage show and 'go to London to studios there and be groomed for stardom'. My parents knew nothing of this world, and I must have caused them a great deal of anguish and anxiety, for I so desperately wanted to go. The other problem was that my schooling hadn't been completed. My parents went to see the headmaster of the Academy to discuss my leaving. There was a great to-do about it all, the headmaster saying I would be sorry if I left school early; but finally I went. Before I left home my father and mother gave me a Bible to take with me, with an inscription inside, and my father said, 'As long as you remember, Jenny, to stay the way you are and come back to the house the way you left it.'

He was particularly worried that I might be led astray, and even start to drink. I promised him that I wouldn't touch any alcohol. His influence on me was so strong that to this day I have never had any desire to drink. Sometimes, when people say to me, 'Here you are, just a little something to give you a lift or keep you calm', I'm very glad that my love of the theatre and the happiness I feel when I work give me all the lift I need.

I soon found out that all the talk of 'stardom' was just nonsense. Each week I kept expecting a call to London and the bright lights, but no call came. The show was pretty tatty – it included other boys and girls in their teens, and a matron to look after us. We toured Scotland and England in second- and third-rate theatres. I had been told that I would have special material written for me, but that was nonsense too, and I ended up putting my own bits and pieces together. One never-to-be-forgotten night, we sat backstage after the show on our suitcases, unable to leave the theatre because the manager had gone off with the takings.

We travelled from place to place in an old coach. It was very cramped, and I remember the big bass fiddle slung right down the centre. The reason I remember it so well is because on one occasion I stood up, the coach gave a lurch, and the long steel spike of the fiddle that usually goes into the stage went into my coat and ripped it right down the back. I expect at the time I wondered what on earth my mother would say.

I kept a diary, which I found in the loft not so long ago. It's full of sad little lines like 'Had herrings for tea. Hope there are more people in the theatre tonight.' I was certainly beginning to find out what theatrical life was all about!

After three months with the show, my parents came and fetched me home. One of my relations had been to see it at her local theatre and felt it was far from the right place for me to be. She wrote to my parents, saying how upset she was to see me in such a set-up. Although I realize it was all for my good, at the time it broke my heart. Each day I looked for letters from the company that never came, and I think now that what I was experiencing was the nearest thing to a breakdown. Sitting in the bedroom with the most desolate feeling inside me, I missed the theatre dreadfully and didn't know what was going to take its place. I had to have a job.

That job turned out to be in the local Co-op. I couldn't stand the thought of sitting all day at a desk: an office was not for me, and when my mother took me round for an interview with the manageress of the shop, Miss Munro, it was agreed I would start in the baby department. I was still only fourteen – which often makes me wonder, when I look at my own daughter, how I could have left home at such an early age thinking I was perfectly capable of looking after myself! It's a hair-raising thought, and says a lot for the trust my parents put in me.

Working in the Co-op wasn't what I'd wanted to do, but everyone was kind to me and I really enjoyed learning how to be a good shop assistant. When I first started there I was self-conscious about the fact that I was working in a shop when some of my friends had taken jobs in offices. If I was outside washing the windows, complete with my brush and pail, and saw them coming from the train from Glasgow I'd dash back inside. Sometimes I had to take a parcel of clothes to Miss Stanage who lived down the main street and did the alterations. I hoped like mad I wouldn't see any of them, otherwise it meant hiding in a close.

My trips to Miss Stanage could be quite an adventure. Whenever I staggered into her room with my enormous brown paper parcel, I had to be sure and close the door firmly behind me. I had been warned that the cat mustn't get out, and that it was very fierce. This made me terribly nervous, and as I carefully placed the parcel on the sofa the cat watched me from across the room with an evil eye. I was terrified it would pounce. And of course it did get out one day. Miss Stanage, who was of a comely build, pushed past me, throwing one of her alterations over it as it made to flee down the stairs – but it still scratched all up her arm.

I can't sew, or cut straight, but when I moved to the ladies' department I helped pin things up for the alterations before taking them to Miss Stanage. There was a funny little wooden gadget that blew chalk round the hem of the dress to mark it level. Then you pinned it up. One woman came in and chose a black dress and asked for it to be altered so that it would be ready for the funeral when the person died!

It's curious, isn't it, you can search back in your mind trying to remember things – some moments remain very clear and others escape you completely. I was reminded of this the other day when a letter arrived out of the blue from someone who had worked in the Co-op asking, 'Do you remember coming up to the office and impersonating the boss? You gave us the fright of our lives!' Well, I'm afraid I don't remember that at all. I wish I did. On the other hand, I do recall how much I liked being sent upstairs to fetch things from the office and while I was there sitting down at the switchboard with all its little numbers clicking away and the cords you had to plug in to connect one call to another. It was great fun. Apart from my visits to the office, I also enjoyed taking myself round to the other departments in the store – to the ladies' and men's wear, and downstairs to the hardware. No wonder Miss Munro shouted so often: 'Jenny Broon, get back to your coonter!'

It was around this time that I applied to the BBC in Glasgow. I was given time off from my work to audition; this was taken from my pay at the end of the week! I earned the princely sum of ten shillings, and when Friday nights came along, I'd hear 'Here's your pay packet, Jenny,' and sixpence would have been deducted if I'd had time off.

I failed my first audition, and was told to go away and do

something about my accent. I don't know what kind of accent
I had but, nothing daunted, I applied again. And this time I
passed. I can see myself now – standing in front of the
microphone, and a voice that seemed to come from nowhere
telling me what to do. It gave me such a fright. In those days,
there was no question of someone in the control room
twiddling knobs and readjusting any sound problem. There
were white circles on the floor, and you stood nearer or further
away from the mike, depending on the instructions you got.
My favourite impression at that time was of Cicely Court-
neidge. I'd seen her at the Alhambra Theatre in Glasgow in
the musical *Under Your Hat*. I thought she was wonderful. She
had this marvellous ability to make the audience roar with
laughter, and then just as quickly, move them to tears. So
there I stood, singing her song 'Gentlemen, the King', doing
her funny laugh, and saluting every time I came to the line,
'Gentlemen, the King'. I don't know how many times I sang
the song for them, but I do know I saluted every single time.
And that was radio!

I can't remember which was my first broadcast after passing
the audition. I think perhaps 'Children's Hour'. I played a
character in some sketch. Later on came other parts in various
drama productions. I wonder if you can imagine what it was
like for me working in the shop busy selling baby garments or
whatever to a customer, and then being called away to answer
the phone, and finding it was the BBC on the line. Could I
accept an engagement on such and such a date? It was
tremendously exciting, nerve-wracking too, because each time
this happened I had to knock on my boss's door and ask
permission for time off. But she was very good about it. Of
course, the sixpence still came out of my pay packet! I loved
these phone calls, never knowing what they might bring, and I
still get excited and delighted when something good is
suggested to do with work – a television show, a cabaret – it
doesn't matter. To be working is the thing.

Perhaps because of the rough times, gratitude figures a
great deal in my life: for good theatres, decent dressing-rooms,
first-class lighting and orchestra. The joy of having my own

trio travel with me remains undiminished. No more 'Let's see your music then,' or 'That's all the time you can have to rehearse,' at band calls.

But back to the Co-op days. If I was gaining experience in broadcasting, I was also gaining experience as a shop assistant. At the beginning, tying a parcel presented great difficulties. It was to do with being left-handed. I was shown how to take the string round, where to place the slip-knot – 'Round this way, do you see? Then like that, and there you are. Now you do it, Jenny.' So I'd do it, and we'd both watch the string fall off the parcel and on to the floor. After several patient efforts it dawned on my instructor that whereas she started with her right hand, I started with my left. No wonder I got in such a mess. To learn more, I was sent round all the departments, selling baby bootees one moment, and silk stockings the next. I definitely didn't like working in the men's wear department – especially if a man wanted trousers and I had to take his inside leg measurements. I hated that! I usually called for Richard, head of the department, to take over for me.

I had been christened Janet, but everyone called me Jenny. I think Jenny is a lovely name now, but at that time I disliked it intensely. It was the way the customers said it: 'I want a raincoat for the wee yin, Je-enny.' They took ages to get the word out, such a long, drawn-out, sound. 'No-oh, that's no big enough, Je-enny. Gie us a look at that yin, Je-enny.'

One day I couldn't stand it any longer. I ran into the cupboard where the stock was kept and breathed 'Bugger, bugger, bugger!' into a shoe-box, and then came out smiling and saying, as I handed yet another new coat to her, 'Would you like to try this one?' It was while serving this customer and listening to her stretch out my name in her usual awful tones that I had a rush of blood to the head and said, 'I've decided I am going to be called Janet.' 'Listen, Je-enny,' she answered, 'you've been Je-enny to me since you were a wee lassie, and you'll be Je-enny tae the end o'yer days.' That made up my mind, and I told everybody, 'Unless you call me Janet, or Jan, I won't answer you.' When I started doing concerts around Glasgow, I used 'Jan Brown' as my billing, but people thought I was a Polish singer, so I packed that in very quickly! I think I was also bothered that I would perhaps be called 'wee Jenny Brown'. Somehow that had the sound of a kilted tap-dancer, and I didn't fancy it.

One morning the phone in the shop rang and I ran to pick it up – oh good, it was the BBC again. This time they wanted me to sing with Ronnie Munro's dance orchestra. Now, I've told you how nervous I felt about singing. But this time was different. The songs were to be bright and bouncy, and besides that they said I could add a little bit of comedy. I did this by re-writing nursery rhymes and performing the verses in different accents. When I finally left the Co-op, the back of the order book was full of my scribbles for all the scripts I had been trying to write. One of the big highlights of working with Ronnie Munro and his orchestra was his appearance at the Glasgow Empire. He played the week there, and I did too – my very first time in a number one theatre. What a thrill! My mother had made me a beautiful new dress, deep blue organdie with traces of gold, and I felt wonderful. The girls I worked with at the Co-op were marvellous. They clubbed together and on the last night of the show they presented me with a bouquet. There was no jealousy or resentment amongst them, they were just terribly pleased for me, and they certainly let me know it as they cheered me on.

The Stage Manager at the Empire was Harry Whiston. After I came off from doing my act he held me by the arm at the side of the stage – held me back really, then pushed me on at just the right moment to take the lovely applause. I took my call – went off to the side, the prompt corner, and again he held my arm. 'Not yet, not yet . . .' he whispered. '*Now!*' He pushed me on. Later in my career I found that it is a great art, the ability to time your applause, although the audience are not aware of it. Some artistes are absolute geniuses at this and I've heard applause at the end of an artiste's act that had started as almost nothing and been turned into a triumph.

I've always had great difficulty in actually 'hearing' my applause – at least this was the case in Variety – and would often think I had died a death. I'd make for my dressing room only to have the Stage Manager run after me shouting, 'Go back go back – can't you hear the applause?' I'm not on my own in this respect. When I toured with the Goons, Harry Secombe would come off stage, the sweat pouring down his face. As he mopped it with a towel he would say in his strong Welsh accent, 'Was I all right then?' while the audience was going mad. He is the most generous performer and the only artiste I can think of who called off to the wings for others to come on stage and share his ovation.

Those of you who ever saw Donald Peers will know he was brilliant at taking calls. I appeared with him once in a Sunday night concert at the Floral Hall, Scarborough. He had completed his act and the orchestra was playing his signature tune 'By a Babbling Brook'. He had left the stage and the curtain had come down. He waited, the applause grew. 'Hold it' he called to the Stage Manager, then 'Now', and up went the curtain again at exactly the right moment to build the applause into an insistent demand for more. This was repeated several times and he finally finished to stamping, whistling and cheering. It really is a wonderful art, the art of timing, and he certainly had it.

I mentioned concerts earlier – well, I did loads of these around Glasgow, all amateur ones, at town halls in Hamilton, Renfrew or wherever. After I had finished my work at six o'clock, I'd dash home, have my tea, then pack my case. Silver shoes in first, next my music, and finally, carefully folded in tissue paper, the dresses my mother had made. They were very pretty. I remember one in pale green taffeta with lovers' knots around the hem, and these were picked out with little bits of diamanté. It had a diamanté belt, and by the end of the week I could slide it round my waist easily, because I'd lost so much weight. Picking up my case and ukelele, I was off, usually by bus. Even then I always seemed to be packing and going somewhere. But it was wonderful experience, and I learned a great deal.

You often hear the question 'Where can up and coming artistes try out their material now?' It's not easy. Things have changed such a lot – people are entertained in front of their own television sets instead of going to a town hall concert. But there are still local shows, and other avenues that weren't around then. Holiday camps, for example – look at the number of artistes who have gained their experience that way: amongst others, Jimmy Tarbuck and Des O'Connor. I think as a starting point anything local is best: if there's a local radio station or you feel ready to apply to the BBC, take a chance – go ahead and do it, you can't wait for it to come to you. Sometimes in conversation I hear a person being asked, 'Would you like to be in the theatre?' And they reply, 'I wouldn't mind.' That's no good – you either want to, and it's an overwhelming want, or you don't. It's only because you *want* to that you can accept and cope with so many of the hard times. Theatre people are great. They have a capacity to take a heart-breaking situation, especially when it concerns themselves, and turn it into one of the funniest stories you've ever heard. It's their survival kit, really.

Going back to the concerts I was telling you about: there was one that was very special for me because the top of the bill was the great Scottish comedian, Sir Harry Lauder. He was an old man by then, and everyone was very much in awe of him. I had been told he was extremely fussy about who went on before him. Usually at these concerts I was the only young artiste, the rest of the programmes generally consisted of perhaps a violinist, a straight singer and a conjurer. I felt awfully nervous when I met him, but he had no objection to me preceding him. I felt very honoured. I don't remember much of what he did, but one thing stuck in my mind. He sang one of his best-known songs, 'I love a lassie', and started to unwrap the engagement ring he was going to give her. The unwrapping went on and on, the paper growing longer and longer, but he held the audience completely, they were quite happy to wait. Another thing he did when he sang was to put 'Oh aye – heh, heh!' in between verses. I'm not sure if it happened originally to cover a laugh from the audience that never came, or if it was just part of the style then, but I've heard lots of Scottish comedians do it.

During these concerts, I began to find out what stage nerves were all about. Probably because, as the shows became more professional and important, I realized more what I was doing. I vividly remember standing at the side of the stage waiting to go on and having the most awful butterflies in my tummy. They didn't go away – in fact, with each show they became worse. I was learning about following another artiste – the desire to do as well as they did, or even better, listening to their applause and hoping there wouldn't be less when I'd finished my act! I suppose what I'm really saying is that I was learning the meaning of competition.

In 1939 war was declared. There had been lots of rumours that there was going to be one, and I'd heard my parents anxiously discussing my brother Bill and the likelihood of him being called up. Then, suddenly, it seemed as though everything was going to be all right. I have memories of seeing that now-famous newsreel, with Mr Chamberlain, the Prime Minister, returning from Germany, waving a piece of paper signed by Hitler and saying all was well. I recall his broadcast when he announced, 'We are now at war with Germany,' his voice sounding paper-thin and tired.

Shows for the troops were soon being organized by a very energetic newspaper man, Archie McCullloch, and I found myself taking part in them. Archie was always full of enthusiasm, and once more I was to be seen hurrying home from the shop and packing my case. As the war proceeded and the air raids started, so topical lines appeared on the scene. I wonder who starts them? Like the man calling to his wife as he dashed to the air raid shelter, 'Don't bother to go back for your teeth, it's bombs they're dropping, not pies!' And another as rationing came along: the woman who went into a fish shop and said, 'I'd like a pound of whale meat, and would you save the head for my cat?' Catch phrases were the thing. Perhaps the most famous was that of Rob Wilton: 'The day war broke out . . .'

In Rutherglen we experienced very few air raids. 'Air raids'. The words conjure up all kinds of pictures for me. The nights we all dreaded, when the moon seemed to light up everything around us more clearly than we'd ever known. The blinds and curtains drawn, and the ARP warden shouting, 'Put that light out!' if someone had carelessly left a window uncovered. When the air raid sirens sounded in the middle of the night it was a quick dash to find something warm to put on over your nightie and then down the three flights of stairs to huddle in the close with all the other neighbours. I read women's magazines avidly, the beauty page particularly. They were full of instructions about what to wear if you had to go to an air raid shelter: 'Wear an attractive chiffon scarf tied in a bandeau to hide your curlers,' and 'Don't forget to put on a pretty lipstick – learn how to do this in the dark.' I thought it was great stuff, but there never seemed to be time to do it. Although there was one very bad raid when Clydebank was mercilessly bombed, Scotland never experienced the horrors that the rest of the country knew. And I don't think in the early days people at home were all that much affected by the war. It may sound heartless, but women still queued up on a Saturday for their cream cakes from the bakery and wondered what they would cook for Saturday tea.

One of the most popular radio shows was 'Henry Hall's Guest Night'. Everyone listened to it. First the signature tune, and then Henry's voice: 'This – is Henry Hall speaking', with that slight hesitation he had – 'and tonight – is my guest night.' Everyone knew that phrase. When I appeared with Ronnie Munro and his Scottish Variety Orchestra at the Usher Hall in Edinburgh, the positions were reversed and Ronnie was able to introduce Henry Hall as his guest. He was charming and courteous, and was referred to by the musicians either as 'Mr Hall' or 'the guv'nor' – never Henry. They had great respect for him. I recollect little about the show except the surprise of working on a stage with people seated not only in front of you, but behind you as well. Quite a strange feeling, trying to perform all the way round, it made you feel rather like a lighthouse.

The next day there was a ring at the bell, and when Mother opened the door, there was Henry Hall – tall, grey-haired and bespectacled. My mother had no idea who he was, and said rather sharply when he introduced himself, 'Just let me dry my hands, I'm rinsing some washing out in the bath.' The reason for his visit, he explained, was that he had watched me in the show and liked what I'd done, and wanted me to join him and his orchestra on tour. It seemed hardly real! Henry Hall here in my lobby, in Rutherglen. His was the top radio orchestra in the country. Theatres were packed to capacity wherever they played. I knew it meant being in all the number one theatres throughout the country with a first-rate company. It is difficult to put into words that elated, excited feeling you experience when you are offered something suddenly out of the blue. I always think it's only theatre people who know this, but I'm probably quite wrong. That leap from nothing happening, to everything happening.

Oh, how I wished the answer to Henry's request could have been yes, but it was too late. I told him that because I didn't want to work in a munitions factory, I had volunteered for the ATS, that my papers had gone and that I was just waiting on word from the Army. When he heard this, he said he would see what he could do, and after I received my call-up papers for preliminary training at Dalkeith outside Edinburgh, I was told that the War Office in London wanted to see me. Henry had been as good as his word and had written to Major Basil Brown who was head of Combined Services Entertainment for the forces.

My papers for the ATS finally arrived and, full of expectancy, I prepared to leave home. My mother and father were so good about everything, though I expect they were relieved to hear that I was only going as far as outside Edinburgh to start with. I don't remember any tears, just great excitement on my part and an eagerness to know what this new life was going to be like. The girls in the Co-op gave me a brown leather shoulder bag which I loved and later on wore proudly with my uniform. But as the song says, let's start at the very beginning . . .

3

So This Is The Army

Being in the ATS was quite an experience. I was given an aptitude test to see if I was suitable to be a driver. What squares didn't go into what round holes – you know the sort of thing. I could have saved them the bother. I've never been able to cope with what I call gadgets – even opening a packet of Lux is a traumatic event. Somewhere in Robert Benchley's writing there's a line about the struggle with inanimate objects – that's me trying to open a case! You will have gathered from all this that I wasn't given the job of driver. I ended up sitting at a telephone switchboard. Shades of my days at the Co-op, and much more my cup of tea.

Many of the girls I met up with were deeply homesick and hated it all, and when we queued up with our billy-cans and a weird concoction of baked beans, bacon, fried bread, anything that was around, was plonked into them, everything together, it was more than they could cope with. The last thing they wanted to do was eat, and so I would often eat theirs as well as mine. The kitting out was the best part. I thought it hilarious to see these girls with stockings twisted and drooping round their ankles; one would be wearing a hat that was too small, sitting on top of her head like a pea on a dumpling, another a jacket too large with sleeves hanging down. But it was those knickers – they had to be seen to be believed! Khaki-coloured, enormous they were. No wonder they were labelled 'passion-killers'! Mind you, though I laughed hysterically at the sight of us all, I was well aware that I was one of them. Out of one hut into another we marched, trying on shoes, the laces still

50

undone, pulling on shirts with no time to button them: relentlessly we carried on until eventually we all had a complete uniform. So here I was – Private J. Brown. Wearing a khaki shirt, dark tie, straight Army-coloured skirt ... I was very smart. In fact I must have looked highly efficient behind the desk in the office, because on one occasion a private came in, saw me and immediately leaped to attention and saluted. For a moment I thought there was someone behind me.

'Get your hair off your collar,' was a command I heard many times during my training. This was bellowed by fierce-looking women sergeants who seemed to take enormous pleasure in frightening the life out of us. But really when all the marching up and down took place, with shouts of 'Swing those arms! Keep your heads up!', I thoroughly enjoyed it.

Eventually, when my posting came through, it was to go to London and the War Office. I was terribly excited about it all and between the train journey and not eating much, as well as lugging my heavy kit-bag up and down the tube station steps, I finally arrived at the ATS transit building in Gower Street absolutely exhausted. When the officer in charge asked me crisply, 'Where have you come from?', I went blank. I couldn't remember for a few minutes where I'd come from. I was so gone, I didn't know what day it was.

The next morning I reported to the War Office, and to Major Basil Brown. He was a bluff, friendly man with slightly protruding teeth, and he explained how he had heard all about me from Henry Hall, and that in the Army there were shows called 'Stars in Battledress', did I know anything about them? No, I did not. Well, these shows consisted of soldiers, all of whom were artistes in civilian life and who had been taken from their jobs in the Army to make up concert parties. They generally consisted of six or seven men, and they toured all over the country giving performances to all the Services. So far these shows had comprised only men, but now he had an idea to introduce women into them. It was to be an experiment, and this was where I would come in. Would I give it a try and see whether I liked it and, what was even more important, whether the men would mind a girl touring with them? I didn't hesitate, it was a new venture and I was keen to try it out.

The next step was to report to the Duke of York's Barracks on the King's Road, Chelsea. This was the headquarters of the Central Pool of Artistes. The commanding officer was Captain George Black Jnr., son of the great impresario George Black, who presented so many West End stage successes.

The following morning I duly presented myself at the Duke of York's Barracks, and climbed the stairs to the office. It was a hive of activity. Soldiers passed me with sheaves of papers, hurrying as if they might miss the last train; huge skips containing heaven knows what lay with their basket mouths open. It was all very exciting and interesting. And then I was taken to meet Captain George Black. He was a man of average height, slim, had a little dark moustache – I always thought of him as very like David Niven. But most of all he was charming and kind. I must have looked so lost in that office, surrounded by people who all seemed to know what they were doing, whereas I had no idea! It wasn't long before I found out. I had no glamorous stage dresses, knew little about make-up, but all this was soon taken care of. First my dresses: appointments were made for me to meet Alex Shanks, who was one of the leading West End designers at that time. Captain George Black always tried to get the best for you.

I loved the dresses that were designed for me – one was in pale blue chiffon with a heart-shaped neck, puffed sleeves and a marvellously swirling skirt, which I found later I could pick up and move in a very film-starrish way. It delighted me when I took my calls; I had never worn such a dress. Another in red had a square neck rather like a gym-slip, and under it he designed a beautiful white organza blouse with frilled sleeves *à la* Carmen Miranda, edged with red. I was told to take care of these dresses; everything had been budgeted for and they had to last for a long time.

Sergeant-Major Stanley Hall would take care of my make-up. In civilian life he had been a top make-up man at Denham studios. Can you imagine what all this was like for me – a girl from Scotland, with no real stage background, suddenly in the midst of all these professional people? Sergeant-Major Hall was a fine tall man, six foot two at least; he spoke with a Yorkshire accent and his smile was warm and welcoming. He was marvellous to me, showed me how to make up properly, teaching me the little tricks such as glueing the edge of the false eyelashes to the outer edge of the eyelid to get an open- not a closed-eye look, and to line the inside of the lower part of your eye with a light liner to make your eyes look much larger. They were all such useful hints to someone like me just starting, and many artistes have been grateful for his help. After the war, along with his partner Captain Noel McGregor who was also at the Central Pool of Artistes, he ran Wig Creations in Portland Mews. They specialized in the making of wigs for stage and screen, supplying West End shows, film studios and even the Metropolitan Opera House, New York. His salon walls were lined with photographs of all those he had worked with, and there are many well-known actors and actresses who have benefited from his cleverness and to whom he gave a glamour they would otherwise never have possessed. A really lovely man, he has remained one of my friends throughout the years and is as kind and helpful now as he was then.

I was to discover that all problems in connection with the shows, such as the replacing of props, and the placing of artistes to different companies of 'Stars in Battledress', were all dealt with from this office. Many famous names made their way in and out of this building – Terry-Thomas, Charlie Chester, Peter Ustinov, Bryan Forbes, and many, many more, all of course in their Army uniforms. I've tried hard to remember where I first joined my 'Stars in Battledress' company; I think it was in Aldershot. I recollect Stanley making me a long trailing hair piece, as my hair was short because of Army regulations. It was fixed to a tape, the idea being to give me luxuriant locks. I am afraid I didn't quite understand how this should go on, so I just tied it round on top of my hair. I later found out it should have gone on under my own hair and been curled in. The look I achieved was strange, to say the least, and goodness knows what the audience thought – for each time I turned my head the hair piece swung round and hit me smartly in the face.

It was natural that the company should be wary of me – after all, they had a highly successful show, and now I had come along. Was I going to destroy the balance of things? I hoped not, and was anxious to fit in. It was all different for me too, the only girl in a company of six men. I was talking to Alan Clare recently – he was the pianist in the show – and he said, 'You know, Jan, it was a bit like Snow White and the Seven Dwarves. We became fiercely protective about you.'

The show was made up of singer Don Carlos, who was so well-known then for his radio programmes with Troise and his Mandoliers; Boy Foy, a brilliant juggler who juggled effortlessly as he tore round the stage on a uni-cycle – he had appeared many times at the London Palladium as a top variety act; then there was Bert Scrace, a song and dance man – he was always complaining about having flat feet! Jack Browning, a light comedian from West End musicals with a very caustic wit; and Alan Clare, whom I have already mentioned. His piano playing was so sensitive, and to have him accompany me was a joy. Finally, to keep all this lot in order was Sergeant Harold Childs. He had been part of a highly successful stage act called the Three Loose Screws and looked after me like a father. I was delighted to find I'd been accepted, that there had been no question of a request that I be sent back to London, and so I started in with all the boys, touring the Army camps, travelling in style in the back of a three-ton Bedford truck, sitting on the hard metal seats which ran along each side, or on top of a skip – for all the props went with us and we just used whatever was available. I was wonderfully happy, and terribly young in outlook. Well, I *was* young, I wasn't yet twenty-one – but I really mean I was very naive, blushed easily and was always being teased by the others in the party. They laughed at my Scottish accent. In one of the canteens they heard me ask, 'Can I have a cup of tea and a ham sangwich?' That was it – to my bewilderment they kept repeating, 'Anyone for a hang sangwich?' What was wrong, I asked. Harold looked at me with great amusement.

'It's *sandwich*, not sangwich . . .!' Another word they latched on to was film. I talked about going to see 'a smashing filum' and 'a lovely filum star'. '*Film, film*, not filum!' And there was another one. 'I like cream carmels . . .' 'No, no, it's *caramels*.' This was the start of my lessons on how to speak English. I suppose I was a kind of Scottish Eliza Doolittle! When I returned later to Rutherglen on leave, a neighbour remarked, 'Oh, you've become very Englified!'

The boys were always looking for ways to make me laugh on stage. I wrote songs then – they were terrible, but at the time I thought they were marvellous. Awful, corny lyrics like this one:

> *I take my hat off, boys, to you*
> *I take my hat off, yes I do*
> *The way you do things with a smile*
> *Just seems to make this world worthwhile.*

Isn't that dreadful! To think I had the nerve to stand there and sing this to the troops! Poor troops. It's amazing that we ever won the war. During one performance when I thought I was doing particularly well, I glanced off to the side of the stage, and standing in the wings was my Sergeant and two of the company clad from neck to foot in hideous long-john combinations, wearing top hats! I was happily singing my line 'I love Canadians with their style, I love the Aussies with their smile . . .' – 'The horses . . .?' they mouthed, 'what's all this, "I love the horses with their smile"?' It was no good, I collapsed in laughter. The song soon bit the dust, but the teasing went on. I never knew what was coming next.

When we toured the Army camps in Devon, I was told, 'You've got a marvellous write-up in the *Honiton Cliff Times*, you should go into the local newspaper office and get it.' As usual, I fell for this, and couldn't wait to call and see my fantastic write-up. It was a tiny little place and when the man behind the counter heard my request, he shook his head. 'There's no such paper as the *Honiton Cliff Times*.' 'But there must be,' I insisted, 'I've got a write-up and I want to see it.' Then as I looked out the glass door I saw them all hiding round the corner and waiting with great grins on their faces like some Mack Sennet comedy team. I had a lot to learn! But I knew they teased because they were fond of me. I'm still teased dreadfully even now. One comedian said to me, after telling me some risqué story, 'It's the look of shock on your face, I just can't resist it.' I think it's probably that Scottish upbringing that's responsible.

We did shows every night. These could be in anything from a theatre to a Nissen-type building, travelling often quite long distances in the day, and arriving back at our billets at a very late hour. My billets or digs were never with the boys. Certainly one of the perks of being with 'Stars in Battledress' was not having to stay in Army camps, not having to get up early, and – hooray! – not having to 'Stand by your beds for kit inspection'! But one of the things I definitely didn't consider a perk was the time we had to spend being entertained after the show in the Sergeants' mess, or the Officers' mess. We weren't invited to the Officers' mess too many times: after all, we were only humble soldiers – not like ENSA, whose artistes were automatically given the rank of officer, should they ever be captured! Entering rooms that were, for the most part, hot, noisy and full of smoke filled me with dread. Having to shout to make yourself heard has never been my idea of fun, and propping up the bar held even less pleasure for me. Of course, not all messes were like this, and when they were friendly and quiet I enjoyed it as much as anyone. But it did mean always leaving the camp very late.

On these long journeys we all sat in the back of the truck, hail, rain or shine. I would go blue with cold and have to have my hands thawed out, either before going on stage or when we all finally got out of the truck on our return. I can see that truck now, with its tailboard and the chain to lock it; the canvas flap we let down to keep out the cold or the rain. I loved leaping in and out of the three-tonner – though tight skirts presented a problem. Later I wore trousers – much easier. I was one of the boys. It was all that mattered.

I had lunch with Alan Clare not long ago. His memory about certain events is much better than mine. He reminded me of his concern over my blue hands, and I reminded him of one or two things. He was such a marvellous jazz pianist, but he hated, really hated, the pianos he had to play on, and worried himself sick that thumping away on the stiff keys would ruin his technique. His hatred of the poor instrument had to be seen to be believed. First he would take the front off the piano, then the lid, till eventually the piano was standing stripped naked – not a pretty sight, especially for the audience. I remember him looking at the keyboard of yet another terrible piano – the action had gone because of all the beer that had found its way into its innards from hectic nights in the Sergeants' mess. The keys were in a dreadful state and I was going to rehearse a song. 'What key do you want, Jan?' And with that he picked up a handful and said, 'Take your choice.' Never mind, none of those heavy times have affected his playing, it is as sensitive and brilliant as ever, and out of it all we had some marvellous laughs.

He also jogged my memory on pay parades. Pay parades were a wonderful affair. I remember one classic occasion when I stood in line with all the other members of my company – I was the only girl and I wanted to impress them as to how smartly I could do things. It was recognized that those in 'Stars in Battledress' were something else, and I certainly helped paint the picture. My name was called and I saluted in the ranks, out of the ranks, marched smartly to the table, picked up the money, dropped it, saluted again and marched off the wrong way. I knew I was in the Army, but clearly I was not of it.

Alan asked me at lunch, 'Do you remember the night when we were making our way back to the truck after the performance – it was pitch black, and we suddenly realized you weren't with us? You had fallen down a great deep hole.' Yes, I remembered that. 'But when we got you out, it was a cess-pit you'd fallen in, and nobody wanted to know you.' No, I couldn't remember that part, and I said to Alan that probably the shock wiped it from my mind. 'Don't you remember? An ATS Sergeant kindly took you away and cleaned you up.' No wonder I preferred to forget it!

It's difficult to remember all the impressions I did then. There was of course Mae West, Jessie Matthews, Bette Davis, Katharine Hepburn, Gracie Fields, Vera Lynn, Tessie O'Shea, and there was one film star called Virginia O'Brien, an American singer with a poker face who never moved a muscle when she sang. This was one of my favourites. It's funny really, the format for impressions is still very much the same now as it was then – to find a song with different verses and have different stars sing them. The songs I used then were 'Pistol Packing Momma', and 'Don't Sit Under the Apple Tree', and they went down very well with the audiences. Somewhere along the line I sang as Virginia O'Brien, 'Only a bird in a gilded cage, a beau- . . . a beau- . . . a beautiful sight to see. Shoot the liquor to me Daddy . . .' and up would go one shoulder, while the face remained rigid. It was great fun to do.

In June of 1944 my party followed the invasion forces, and left for France to entertain them there. I wasn't allowed to go, and this upset both me and the boys terribly. We were a team. We went everywhere together, shared all the laughs together, and now I had to be left behind. I joined another company at home, but it wasn't the same. All I wanted to do was to be back with my party, and finally I was told that I could go. Permission had to be given by my parents, for I was still under age, and I realize now how good they were about it all. They must have had many qualms about such an unknown venture, but they said yes.

In August I set off to join my beloved 'Stars in Battledress' party, as usual full of excitement. I was one of four girls – there was a singer and the Tanner Sisters, Stella and Frances. We were the first to go to France to entertain the troops. I soon found out what that meant. Wherever the Army moved, we moved as well. But I'm jumping ahead.

I left for France in a packed troop ship. Where I came ashore I've no idea. Recounting this part of my life is like trying to remember a dream. Even when putting down the things I do recollect, it seems as if I am talking about someone else and not me at all. What I do know is that when I did make contact with my party, they were giving a show to the troops in the middle of a large field. All the soldiers were sitting in rows on the grass, and the boys were using a large table top for a stage. I can certainly remember that, because I'd been brought to where they were, not in a truck but on the back of a motor-bike. It had been quite a long journey on very dusty roads, and I'd been waving cheerfully to all the soldiers I'd passed on the way. It struck me that no one seemed to be in a hurry to wave back. It was only after I arrived that one of the company thought I should have a look in a mirror. I did, and nearly fainted. The face that looked back at me was white with dust, and the hair looked even worse. I know I roared with laughter – no wonder nobody wanted to wave to me! In a way it was the right kind of entrance to make. Dust or no dust they were delighted to see me and I was equally happy to see them. But how to clean up? Someone got hold of an Army blanket and slung it between two trees for me to hide behind. Somebody else found me a biscuit tin which they filled with water, and I proceeded to have a minor bath and to wash that dirt right out of my hair.

Then it was my turn to go on. What a welcome I was given! I suppose the surprise of seeing a girl artiste when they thought there were only men there had a lot to do with it. It was a strange feeling for me, performing outdoors. The wind always seems to carry your voice away, and though we had a microphone it was still tricky. We worked under all kinds of conditions, sometimes using two Army trucks as changing rooms, and with the tailboards down and held together this made an entrance to a basic stage. Boy Foy managed to perform on stages the size of a postage stamp, juggling and cycling, looking immaculate in his Eton jacket and striped trousers, finished off with a shiny top hat. Alan's hatred of the pianos he played and his desire to do something dreadful to them continued. One wonderful night, riding back in the truck along the terrible bumpy roads, as usual surrounded by all the props, he executed his masterstroke. We had been given a mini-piano to travel, which was roped up like a bull at the back of the truck. Suddenly there was a most awful noise –

as the truck went down a hill, so the piano started to move backwards; as we went up a hill, so the piano moved majestically towards the tailboard. He had undone the rope! As we went up one particularly steep hill, the piano sailed past us and with a fiendish yell Alan undid the tailboard flap and it sailed off into the darkness and out into the night. When I reminded him of this he roared with laughter. 'Oh that was a marvellous moment. And do you remember that funny thing you did with your teeth?' My teeth? 'Yes, that gap you had in them, and the candle grease . . .' We were off again! You see, my teeth protruded – they still do – and I had a great gap between the two front ones. I'd forgotten all about this, but I used to painstakingly melt candle grease, standing in the dressing room with my lit candle and letting little bits of it fall into a tin. Then I'd take the grease and I'd mould it into the gap – another of Stanley Hall's helpful hints. From out front I looked as if I had nice even teeth – except the only problem was the little bits that occasionally broke off and went flying into the audience! Whenever I met Army dentists they were intrigued and often asked if they could stand at the side of the stage and see the effect. I was quite a novelty.

As the troops moved up the line, so did we. At one time we completely lost touch with our headquarters and no one quite knew where we had got to. There were no other women around. It's strange, but while I'm writing this I think how often I've been a 'surprise' – as then, when I was hidden away from the troops and suddenly produced, or now, when I unexpectedly appear as Maggie. The surprise I'm thinking about happened when we journeyed through the Falaise Gap. I can still recall the signs by the roadside: 'Verges cleared to four feet' as a warning against land-mines, and from time to time the sound of them exploding in the distance. My company would not let me look out of the truck, because there were dead soldiers lying everywhere. I didn't look, but I have a picture in my mind of dead cows in fields, their stomachs distended, and lying in grotesque positions.

When we reached the camp, I queued up with the others for a cup of tea. The soldier behind the trestle table was stunned when he saw me. 'Let's clean the cup for the lady,' he said, and proceeded to polish it with a filthy tea cloth.

A disused factory was our theatre that time. I was hidden away, and the show started. The place was crammed to the roof with soldiers – they were sitting on beams, hanging from the window ledges – and out of the blue I walked on stage. It was a marvellous moment. The whole audience erupted, and their cheers nearly took the roof off.

It's impossible for me to write about this part of my life in any proper sequence. I didn't keep a diary, and so any moments that come to mind are really more like a series of pictures that I've snapped, put away in the attic and am now coming across again for the first time since then. The picture of a theatre, for example – who knows where? – when the curtains opened and we were faced with a rather different kind of audience – they were soldiers alright, but they were asleep! They had returned from the fighting to this rest camp, and tired though they were they had wanted to see the show and above all to have a good laugh. But it had all been too much for them, and they'd passed clean out.

I think maybe entertainment had its real value for the troops at times like this, and perhaps too from the artistes' point of view we learn a little of our real value. How many times have you felt a bit down, gone into a theatre and been so lifted up by the performance that you go out feeling on top of the world? I know it has certainly happened to me.

Click – another picture. A packed theatre. The comedian telling his funniest stories, but no sooner did a joke begin than the audience laughed uproariously. The comedian reached the end of the gag and there was utter silence. We discovered later, they had understood nothing – they were Polish. And somewhere in my mind is another quick snapshot, this time near Neinmegen. There were no women there at all and the Commanding Officer, Donald Wilson, decided he had better get me back down the line after the show. We drove back in an open Jeep. I was Scottish, so was he – that was it. We sang all the songs we knew at the top of our voices – 'I belong to Glasgow', 'Annie Laurie', 'My Love is Like a Red Red Rose' –

while the stars looked down and the sound of gunfire filled the air. I finally reached a camp where there were some nurses. They didn't have a spare bed, so that night I slept on a stretcher.

But all the constant moving around, travelling long distances, and sometimes starting at ten in the morning and giving as many as five shows a day, suddenly caught up with me. Conditions were very rough, and I remember sitting under a tree one day, trying to dig out of a billy-can some pretty awful looking food without the help of a fork or knife, and feeling sickened by it all. I explained earlier that we had no status of any kind, and while the ENSA companies were usually invited back to the Officers' mess after a performance, we more often than not had to rough it. It was all suddenly too much, and I longed to go home.

One evening, after a performance to the RAF in Brussels, I talked long and hard to an officer, saying how much my company needed a break. In the end, to our amazement and delight, we were informed that they could arrange for us to fly back in a Dakota. I thought it was a Lancaster, but Alan Clare tells me it was a Dakota. I know it had hard metal seats, and we sat facing each other as if about to do a parachute jump. But no discomfort mattered – we were on our way back to London.

I should have felt elated when I returned. Instead, I always seemed to be sitting on top of buses while tears poured down my cheeks. I couldn't stop them. It was explained to me I was having a nervous breakdown, and I was promptly packed off to hospital. Now, apart from a quick do as a child when I had my tonsils out, I'd never had anything to do with hospitals. To see people sitting in bed with bandages on frightened the life out of me. But I was looked after well, and after a fairly short period, I returned to London and was discharged from the Army. It was 1945, and time to begin a different way of life.

4

Pete And I

When I returned to my home in Rutherglen I felt restless. I had to decide what I was going to do – return to the Co-op and the baby department, or take a chance and try my luck on the stage in London. I am sure my mother and father would have much preferred to have me stay at home, and people I met in the main street said, 'I expect you'll be settling down now.' Oh, I didn't like that phrase. Why should I settle down? There was so much to do yet.

During the time I had been in the Army I had taken part in forces broadcasts from the Fortune Theatre. The producer of these programmes was Vernon Harris. One day I received a letter from him at the BBC asking me to get in touch with him. I dashed along to the Post Office at the end of the road and made my call from the phone box there – we had no phone in the house, remember. I suppose this call really made up my mind for me. He told me about a new late-night radio review he intended to do, called 'Cap and Bells', with songs and sketches, and he thought I might like to be in one and to do a short spot of my impersonations. I heard myself saying, 'In one? Oh no, if it's not to do all the series, it's not worth while coming all the way to London.' I laugh when I think about it – what a nerve! I wouldn't dream of saying such a thing now. It's said that ignorance is bliss, and it certainly was in my case. I remember seeing Florence Desmond, the brilliant impersonator, at the Empire Theatre, Glasgow. Oh, I can do that, I thought, but I'll do it better. How little we know when we're beginning! It's only as you watch other artistes and see the

63

amount of study and rehearsing that has gone into their presentation that you begin to realize how much you have to learn. At this time I knew nothing of the whys and wherefores of professional life. I suppose in my practical way I was weighing up the expense of travelling from Scotland to London. I had very little money – in fact, only £29 gratuity from the forces. And Vernon, perhaps taken aback by this reply, agreed to my being in the programme each week.

While I was still at home a review came to Glasgow called *Back Home Again*. There had been a great deal of publicity about it. They had an all-male cast, but that was not what made the show unusual. It was the fact that all the performers had been in Stalagluft III – they were all ex-prisoners of war. I knew about one of them, Squadron Leader Talbot Rothwell, from an ATS girlfriend of mine, Sally Rogers. She had written to him while he was in Germany, and so I went to see him. After the show, which was excellent, full of good songs and sketches, I went round to meet him. He asked me if I'd like to come out to supper, along with one of the others in the company, Lieutenant Commander Peter Butterworth. I had seen him in the show playing a marvellous character called Mrs Wintergreen, a lady who had made a stirring speech about the items her committee were making for 'our dear boys in the forces', including a new type of combination that was 'reinforced' – pause – 'with steel wool' – another long pause – 'I imagine our boys will be tickled to death when they hear about this'. He was very funny, and he looked quite outrageous, dressed in a bright floral silk two-piece with an over-smart straw hat, and teetering about on very high heels.

Several things stand out in my mind when I think back on that evening. We went to a popular Italian restaurant in Glasgow. I was wearing a coat that had seen better days. It had been light in colour, but was now dyed navy blue. The lining had suffered in the dying process, and had done that awful thing that happens with sleeves when they part company from the material. Peter leaned forward as we sat at the table. 'Let me help you with your coat,' and he proceeded to slip it off my shoulders and place it carefully over the back of my chair. Oh, the embarrassment! I knew the lining was in a real old mess, but I said nothing.

The food arrived. They were both so polite, their manners impeccable. During a lull in the conversation the waiter picked up the plates thinking they'd finished. He might have been speared to death, the forks and knives came down so quickly – 'No, we haven't finished, thank you.' They had experienced years of semi-starvation in the prisoner-of-war camp – later I heard of some of the recipes they had made up – but to reject any food was an absolute crime and they were horrified that what was on their plates was about to be thrown out.

When the meal was over, Peter leaned forward again. 'Let me help you on with your coat.' 'Oh, thank you.' I put my arm down the sleeve, only to find it hopelessly tangled in the torn lining. I could have died! But that wasn't the finish. They insisted on getting a taxi and seeing me out to my home in Rutherglen. I was in a high old state. The snob in me had taken over, and the last thing I wanted them to see was where I lived, and stopping the taxi outside the close! If I'd lived in one of the grand avenues, it would have been a different matter. 'Oh, just down here on the left – no, no – there.' 'Oh there,' said Talbot Rothwell, 'where the sign is for Capstan cigarettes?' It was hanging above one of the shops. 'No, no, not there.' At least my close looked a lot better than that spot. And so it taught me to be a bit more honest with myself.

Peter was the quieter one at dinner. He told me later that I never stopped talking. I was still in some way involved with the forces and knew I could stay at the ATS transit camp in Gower Street, but when he heard this he said, 'You must use my flat, we're touring Scotland for several weeks.' I thought it was just a polite remark, but when I went to leave, he called out, 'Wait a minute, you've forgotten to take the key to my flat,' and he handed me the Yale. I was so surprised to find somebody saying something like this and really meaning it that I took the key.

I was in my usual state of excitement when once again I left home for London, but this time it was different. I was now on my own. It was a whole new adventure. I'd always felt strongly that you had to go to London to be accepted, not just stay in Scotland, and this was now going to be put to the test.

I took myself to Peter's 'flat'. What kind of person was he I wondered, vaguely curious as I looked round his room. Amongst other things there was a ballet shoe hanging by its tape from the mantelpiece, loads and loads of books, and a half-used box of cube sugar. This flat was actually a bed-sitter off Baker Street. The housekeeper's name was Rose, and she always screeched with laughter when she told you that she'd just had a bath and Eddie (her husband) had helped her find the soap.

I used the flat for only a few days, then found my own little room in Cheniston Gardens off Kensington High Street. It was on the top floor and it really was minute. I could sit on the divan, lean forward and make my toast, the little gas fire was so near. It had a meter, of course, and since starting this book and looking back on the diaries I kept, I find I had an absolute obsession with the cost of everything. On every page there is a detailed account of what I spent that day. I had to do this, for I had little money. Every penny was accounted for. Big decisions had to be made. Could I afford a hot water bottle? No. I would just shove the kettle down the bed and plug the spout with cotton wool.

Rehearsals for 'Cap and Bells' began. Vernon Harris was a gentle, amusing producer. Patient, too, for I was always popping into his office with my scribbles to let him hear the material I'd put together for the short spot of impressions, and to ask what he thought about the ideas I had. He was helpful and kind, and I was fortunate to have such a good start. He gave me parts to play in the sketches. This was wonderful experience, learning how to really read a script. The leading lady in the review was Elsie Randolph. I loved watching her as she stood at the microphone, script in her hand. She had a way of holding her finger and thumb together as she read her lines, and her pen was always at the ready for any changes that might have to be made. Her hands were very white, she wore beautiful rings, and her nails were a vivid red. I thought she was wonderfully sophisticated. Everybody sounded sophisticated to me. Naunton Wayne was her partner in the show, and at the piano was Harry Jacobson. They all had this West End feeling about them, and my Scottish way and accent seemed to me to stand out more than ever. Again, there were problems with some of my pronunciations. As I said the word raspberry in one of the sketches, there was a long pause, and then from the control room the disembodied voice said 'What was that?' 'Razzberry.' I was off again. 'No, no, Janet. Raspberry. Raspberry.' I don't know how Scottish people feel now when they speak in a room full of English voices, I only know that at the time my voice always seemed to come out flat and plain, to my ears anyway. But I was finding out the English way, and remembering.

You might wonder why it mattered so much, and why not keep a broad Scottish accent. It was another of those fixations I had, that if I had a strong accent I'd only be given Scottish parts to play, and I didn't want to be limited.

Other radio programmes came along. Many of them had studio audiences, and they were done at the old Monseignor Cinema, Marble Arch. I had to have dresses that looked good. Dress agencies were my life-saver, and I wore many an elegant dress with an expensive label which had cost me very little. I used dress agencies for a long time. One of my favourite jackets that I wear now came from a shop that sells marvellous clothes of the Thirties. I remember Gloria Hunniford whispering in the commercial break during her television show, 'What a lovely jacket, where did you find that?' And I was so pleased that the red light lit up on the camera and I didn't have to tell her!

One day, walking down the Haymarket, I met the manager of the Savoy Cinema in Glasgow who had put on the talent shows. Duncan Ross was his name, a mad Scot who was now living in London and writing television scripts. 'Well, Jenny,' – he still called me Jenny – 'what a wonderful surprise! And how is it all going?' I told him about the broadcasts, but that I

wanted very much to do a show in the theatre since it seemed
to me that the way to be seen in London was to take part in a
Sunday night show. We were standing near Her Majesty's
Theatre, and they were holding one that coming Sunday. To
cut a long story short, he fixed it, and I found myself on a bill
full of stars. Some of my friends told me I was silly – I would
either be on so early I would be forgotten about, or on so late
people would no longer notice who was on. I didn't care. I had
made up my mind, and I did it.

The impresario and band-leader, Jack Hilton, was in the
audience (though I didn't know this), and afterwards when I
met him he asked if I'd like to be in the summer review he
planned to put on at the Floral Hall in Scarborough that year.
Naturally I said yes. I was thrilled to bits about the offer. It
would be my first summer show.

At that time I was more or less my own agent, arranging my
contracts and fees with the booking office at the BBC, but
when Jack Hilton asked me to appear at Scarborough, things
changed. I recollect there was an agent called Jack Fallon, who
began looking after my engagements for me. I received word
from the Hilton office saying they would like me to go to the
Hilton wardrobe and be fitted out for costumes. This
wardrobe was in the basement of a building near Marble Arch.
It was run by a large red-haired lady and the whole place
fascinated me. There were rows and rows of rails with all
kinds of costumes from West End shows, hanging in their
different order; sequined leotards and feathered head-dresses;
gowns of chiffon and beautiful crinolines. As I walked round
one of the rails I walked straight into Peter Butterworth, who
was coming round the other way.

'What on earth are you doing here?' I asked in astonish-
ment. 'I'm going to Scarborough for the summer show.' 'So
am I!' We both looked at each other in amazement. 'See you at
rehearsals.' And that's how it all started.

I hadn't taken to him very much the night we'd met in
Glasgow, and had talked mostly to Talbot Rothwell. I later
found Peter hadn't taken much to me either. When rehearsals
got under way, not only was Peter in the cast, but so was

Talbot Rothwell. The two of them spent so much time laughing together that one of the other girls in the cast and myself had a long chat about them, and decided they must be gay!

I was very broke. The broadcasts didn't pay much, and to rehearsals I wore a reversible mac, green on one side and cream on the other. When the time came for us all to go up to Scarborough, there was a general chat about who would go with whom, and Pete asked if I'd like to do the drive up with him in his drop-head sports car. I asked him later why he asked me, and he said it was to find out if I had anything else to wear on a Sunday! It was a marvellous journey. We spent our time putting the hood up on the car, and taking it off, depending on the weather. Sports car and weather were to be very much part of my life from then on, though I had no idea at the time. He was wonderful fun and made me laugh such a lot.

The principal comedian in the show was Bunny Doyle, a very funny northerner with a screwed-up face and a strong accent. He used to come on in a gladiator's outfit, a door-knocker on the breastplate and a lion's tail in his hand. His first words were 'I'll teach lions to argue', then he'd go into his song – 'I'm glad, glad, very, very glad, I'm glad I'm a gladiator' – a quick bash with the door-knocker on the breastplate and on he would sing. Audiences loved him. In the middle of some serious remark he would suddenly stop and say in broad Yorkshire 'Aren't plums cheap?' Silly lines, but they liked it, and I've heard comedians now using the same approach.

We did an old time musical hall together. I sang 'Josh-ua, Josh-ua, Sweeter than lemon squash you are . . .' and spent the rest of the time giggling behind his back. I was given such a dressing-down on my complete lack of professional behaviour, that I learned never to do it again – or hardly ever. There's nothing more off-putting than artistes on stage having a good time amongst themselves, and the audience utterly outside it.

I found myself in Pete's company more and more, and liking him more and more. This bothered me a lot, for I already had a boyfriend in Scotland. I decided it might be wise to have him come to Scarborough to see how he fitted in with my theatrical friends. This boyfriend had suggested that I should give up the theatre and settle in Glasgow. I told Pete all this. He gave me a severe talking to and said I mustn't do it, that my career was very important. Well, the boyfriend came, and I soon realized it wasn't going to work. When he left, I went with him to York where he was catching the train back to Scotland. As it disappeared from view, I thought suddenly, 'I know what I want to do. I want to marry Peter Butterworth.' I tore back to the hotel in Scarborough where we were all staying, ran up the stairs to his room on the top floor, threw the door open and said, 'I know what I want to do, I want to be married to you.' So you see, I never had this experience of the man going down on his bended knee to ask for my hand in marriage. It was the other way round!

We were mad about each other. The days were wonderful – driving round in his open sports car, the sun beating down, and his Fleet Air Arm wings proudly pinned to my blouse. I count myself as one of the very fortunate ones who really know the meaning of the words 'falling in love'. We neither noticed people nor time, we were utterly wrapped up in each other.

A cousin of Pete's came to stay for a few days. 'This is my cousin, Joan Burnett.' I can see her now. She had reddish-gold hair, and wore a striking blue dress that set off her colouring. She was warm and friendly to me, and it was the first time I'd met any of his relatives. But oh, how we neglected her. While she patiently waited for us we were still holding hands and gazing into each other's eyes. It must have driven her mad, but if it did she hid it well. We've remained the greatest of friends.

Talbot Rothwell, whom I now knew as Tolly, and Pete – somewhere along the line I stopped calling him Peter – still laughed a lot together. The bond that they shared from prison camp was a very strong one, and it never changed. Later on, when I met some of the others who had been with them as prisoners of war, I found they all had this special something. It's difficult to define it: they were just different, and when they met up there was this great affection between them all. Someone once said to me in a prison camp you know people as they really are, and perhaps this was it.

My days were filled with happiness. And then one night I came off stage to be told that my father had died. My father, whom I had loved dearly. He had been so loyal to me when I started doing concerts around Glasgow, and I thought of how he had always come and supported me, though typically in his quiet manner he had said nothing. Only when I hurried home full of excitement – 'Oh Dad, everything went really well and I got on great' – he would say, 'I know, Jenny, I was up in the circle. You did fine.'

I had to go home immediately, and be with my mother. Pete travelled overnight with me up to Glasgow and then he went straight back. As he left me, he said I must be brave and try to look after things. When I reached home I learned how my father had collapsed while playing a game on his beloved bowling green. My mother was broken-hearted. Bill was there, and Chris was given compassionate leave – she was now in the ATS – and we all did the best we could. I arranged that my mother should come and be with me for a little while in Scarborough. Then I had to return to the show.

After my father died, I did my shows just for him. Tears never ran down my face at his funeral, but inside me for a long, long time was a great missing, and a longing to have been able to make his life a little easier for him. It was a terribly difficult time, pretending to be cheerful and happy on stage, while inwardly feeling so sad, but Pete was a great comfort to me.

Wandering around the shops one afternoon, we stopped at a jeweller's, and there on a tray was the sweetest little Victorian ring. It had tiny diamond chips and two small rubies. I loved it, and though Pete hadn't enough money with him, I had. So we went in and bought it. I came back to the theatre wearing it with great pride, but when I showed it to the others they didn't really believe my statement, 'We're engaged', and told me to take that prop ring off. I had quite a job convincing them that I really meant it. The wardrobe mistress said I was far too young! 'You could have had all the men around you,' she exclaimed, 'like bees round a honeypot.' I'd never gone around with lots of boyfriends. For one thing the theatre had always dominated everything and secondly, I'd always felt there could only be one person for me. Pete was the one. So there we were. We met in June and were engaged in September.

I made a hurried trip home, really to show off my ring to my relations. Aunt Mary was very upset when she saw how small my engagement ring was. 'Is there a stone missing?' she enquired acidly. And on hearing I was going to marry an Englishman, 'Is a Scotsman not good enough?' I told her that when I married it wouldn't be a big wedding. Her face darkened even more; all hopes of making special paper bags for the wedding cake were dashed to the ground.

When the show finished we returned to London. It seemed crazy for me to be in my little room in Cheniston Gardens and Pete round at his place off Baker Street. We just had to be together. So we said, 'Let's get married next Monday.' And that's what we did. I knew it was terribly soon after my father's death, but I remembered a bit of advice the psychiatrist had given me when I was ill – 'If you want to go ahead and do something because you feel very strongly that it's right, then do it, because all the other obstacles against it will fade in time.' I felt then that if we didn't go ahead I would always be sorry. And as for any problems beforehand, well they did fade away, and my mother and Pete got along famously.

Naturally, it came as a great shock to my family when I asked them to come to London because I was going to get married next week. I remember some problem about church banns and the panic beforehand. But in the end my mother, along with Bill and Chris, arrived in London and Pete and I were married in St Mary's Church, Bryanston Square. It was a beautiful sunny morning, and I was gloriously happy. The practical streak in me had decided me against being a white bride. I thought I would get little use from the dress afterwards, and so I settled for a dark green suit. It had a kind of highwayman-type jacket and slim skirt – terribly expensive, the most I'd ever paid for anything. With it I wore a tomato red hat and carried a beautiful suede bag to match.

I felt wonderful, and sat playing the piano in the sitting room of the landlord's flat at Cheniston Gardens while waiting for the car to collect me. I waited and waited. Finally it came. Pete had been doing the same thing in the church, waiting and waiting. The cars had collected everyone, but forgotten the bride! At one point – so I heard later from Tolly, who was our best man – a horse had come clopping by and as Pete heard the noise he said, 'Is this her coming now?'

There were only a few friends at our wedding, but as I walked down the aisle I suddenly wished the church had been packed. I was just so happy. There's a picture of us coming out after the service – a pigeon flew past and delivered its congratulations all down Pete's collar.

We decided on Denmark for our honeymoon. In the hotel Pete gave me the most beautiful flowers, but when I turned to thank him he had gone. I found him in the corridor going mad with terrible toothache. What a time to have that happen!

5

A Home Of Our Own

Before we'd gone on our honeymoon, Pete had talked about where we would stay when we came back to London. 'How about your place?'

He'd never seen my little room, and I couldn't stop laughing. 'It would never take the two of us.' 'Oh,' said Pete, 'it can't be that small.' 'Well, it is.' And I told him about making the toast while sitting on the divan. That settled it. It would have to be Montague Street, and that's where we started our married life, in one room with a gas ring to cook on. The room was full of Pete's bits. 'Where are mine going to go?' A blank look came over his face, and then, 'Oh, I'll clear some books.'

He had a pantomime that year at Finsbury Park, and I was to play principal girl for the first time at the Adelphi Theatre in *Red Riding Hood* with Nervo and Knox of the Crazy Gang. It was to be my first West End engagement. I often felt later that the part had happened too quickly, that I wasn't quite ready to appear in a big West End show. I had little experience of production. My principal boy was Noele Gordon. It was a winter when there were lots of electricity cuts. The theatres were freezing and people sat out front in the stalls wrapped up in coats and scarves.

Although I played the girl, I did my impressions in the pantomime as well, with children seated round me on stage and, however it was contrived, managing to do a Shirley Temple. Noele was a very powerful principal boy, and she taught me something that has always remained with me. A stage-hand may make a mistake over lighting, microphones, whatever, and you can accept the mistake – once but not twice. As she put it, 'You're the only one in that spotlight and if anything is wrong, it's you that's standing there, no one else. And to the audience, *you*'ve gone wrong.' It was good advice, and after that if an electrician or a stage-hand made his excuses, I never let it slide. When I toured in Variety, like so many other artistes I'd be there in the prompt corner demanding to know what went wrong, and why. The number of times I've heard rows going on in the prompt corner after a performance is nobody's business. That is the difference between Variety and being in a production. In Variety you really are on your own. You say how many microphones you need, what lighting you require, when you want your tabs to open and close. My mother came to a rehearsal once, and said afterwards, 'Oh, Jan, you're awfully bossy.'

What you don't have any say over is where you appear on the bill. I remember following a dog act. Strapped to their backs they had little monkeys, dressed in jockey outfits with tiny little jockey caps on their heads. When their act had finished and the orchestra went into my play-on music, I discovered to my horror that they wouldn't come off the stage, and as the curtains parted, all you could see were dogs diving round the side drapes, with these strange little monkeys wobbling about on their backs, and the stage hands madly trying to catch them. Through all this my voice could be heard singing off-stage 'We'll build a stairway to the stars . . .'

All during our pantomime run, Pete and I hurried back to our little room off Baker Street. We sat in front of the gas fire while I juggled pots and pans on our one gas ring to try and make us a meal. We had such a lot to share, and we both cared so much about each other's career. When the pantomime finished, I was offered the summer at the Gaiety Theatre, Ayr in Scotland. It was to be a long season, twenty-two weeks. Pete wanted me to take it because it was a good engagement, but I hated the thought of being separated from him.

By this time we had moved from our one room to a little one-bedroomed flat in Praed Street. We had an amazing cleaning lady who came once a week. Her name was Mrs

Trousers. Mrs Trousers was a very large lady who hailed from Scotland and found great difficulty remaining on her feet, breathing heavily and always ready to chat. We had to keep whipping the chairs from under her, for as soon as she caught sight of one she'd sit down and that was the end of the cleaning! I was surprised to be told by her that the air in Pitlochrie didn't agree with her husband, and since coming to London he had breathed much easier. Well, as they say, it takes all sorts.

The night before I left for Scotland we were both miserable. It was going to be terribly hard to be separated, and so far away from each other. Pete was to be in Brighton in a Jack Hilton review. We couldn't have been further apart, but we had agreed, back in Scarborough, we would not try and work together. It could make for difficulties – managements might want one and not the other. Much as I'd wanted to be married to him, I'd felt very strongly that I must keep my independence, and had said anxiously, 'I don't need to change, do I? I'll still be able to do my stage work?' Pete had reassured me that nothing would change.

The star of the show at the Gaiety Theatre, Ayr was the Scottish singer Robert Wilson, who was a tremendous favourite with the Scottish audiences. He had a splendid appearance, with fair hair and the brightest of blue eyes, and he really knew how to 'wear the kilt', as they say in Scotland. His music would start, and he would enter from upstage. Then, with his thumbs tucked into his wide leather belt and his head thrown back, he would fill the theatre with the strains of 'Down in the Glen'. Standing with his thumbs in his belt was a typical stance of Robert's, and I eventually did an impression of him in the show, both of us standing together as we sang 'Westering Home'. He was a tireless worker, but a quiet one, and the public rarely knew just how much he did for charity. We visited a great many hospitals, giving shows in the wards. I thought the world of him. He roared with laughter, I remember, when I told him I'd been given a cookery book called *250 Ways to Cook Potatoes*, but mine always seemed to turn out just boiled!

My feelings at that time were very mixed. I was unhappy at the separation from Pete, but I was also very happy to be on stage. I was constantly torn between the two. Pete and I wrote to each other every day, and oh, the phone calls! I didn't know then that this was how it was going to be throughout our marriage, always endless phone calls from stage doors.

In one of Pete's letters to me that I read again recently he wrote, 'We will never ever be separated for this long again.' By the time the show finished it was into November. I was now desperate to come home. But Pete, thinking of my career, rang one night to say I'd been offered some Moss Empire dates by Jack Hilton, how good it would be for me and that I must accept. I didn't want to, I just wanted to be with him, but I ended up by finishing the summer show, and opening immediately at the Empire Theatre, Edinburgh.

The top of the bill was an American singer, who spoke to no one. He kept his dressing-room door firmly shut, and it was a pretty lonely week backstage. You generally find that when the top of the bill is friendly, with a door that's open to the rest of the cast, there's a happy feeling backstage. It works its way right down the bill, and there's a lovely warm atmosphere.

I know I am lucky to have been part of the Variety period. There were so many artistes to watch from the side of the stage after you'd finished your act. There was Max Miller – we worked together at the Hippodrome, Golders Green. He'd followed me (that is, he came on after me) and as I waited for my cue, he would come up and say, ''Urry up, Janet, don't take too long, girl, I wanna catch the last train back to Brighton' – that's where he lived. Working with him was superb. Halfway through his act he would take a chair, and then sit there strumming a few notes on the guitar, those wicked blue eyes of his picking out some woman in the audience – 'Ain't that luvley, lady, ain't that luvley? Eh, d'you like that? Shall I do it again, eh?'

Max was known to be a very – I won't say mean – careful man. He appeared in Eastbourne one time, and Pete went backstage afterwards to see him. When they came out of the theatre stage door Max pointed across the road to a beautiful

Rolls Royce standing in the forecourt of the hotel opposite – it must have cost him a fortune. 'What d'you think of that then, ain't it luvley?' Just then the rain came down in buckets and Pete asked, 'Shouldn't you have it under cover in the garage?' 'What?' he replied. 'And pay five bob a bleedin' night?'

When I finally finished the tour and came home, it was to another flat, this time a basement in Belgrave Road. Because we'd married the way we did, quickly and without many people being aware of it, we had no long list of wedding gifts – far from it. In Baker Street we'd had to borrow cutlery from the caretaker, and now in Belgrave Road things were pretty much the same. I'd asked two of the company – Jack Barton, who was the producer of the show in Ayr, and Yvonne his wife (she was a lovely dancer and he'd married her after the end of the season) – to come to the flat for breakfast. (Jack's name has been attached to *Crossroads* for many years as a producer, and crazy though it is we've never met up since those early days.) He and Yvonne sat in great style on orange boxes in the kitchen of the flat, while we put together good old bacon and eggs. Nothing mattered – I was home and I was with Pete again.

Sometimes I think about how I've always called him Pete, never Peter. Except if I got angry about something, and then he would say, 'Yes, Janet' – not Jan – and that would make me laugh again. Many of my friends don't seem to like their husbands' names being abbreviated. I wonder why? If you say 'How's Bob?' they say 'Oh, Robert's fine.' 'How's Dick getting on?' 'Oh, Richard's doing very well.'

There was no shortage of engagements, and soon I was being asked to accept more and more Variety work. Pete, on the other hand, was finding it terribly hard. He was an actor – he didn't have an 'act' like me – and things began to get difficult. The times an envelope would land on the mat, and I'd pray it was a contract for him, not for me. Eventually, he was put forward for a part in the film *The Wooden Horse*, the story of the big escape from Stalagluft III. Surely he must be in that film – after all, he spent nearly five years in the camp, and had even taken part in the actual vaulting over the horse and the organizing of the escape. But when he met the casting director he was told he didn't look like a prisoner of war! It was heart-breaking. But as everybody who loves the theatre life knows, it's the hanging on that counts, and Pete hung on. 'I've been offered a part in a film – well, one line actually. What do you think?' 'Oh, I'm sure it could lead to something else – take it.' And so it went on. Television auditions had failed – he didn't have the right face for TV. What could have been more wrong!

Finally, the producer Leslie Jackson glimpsed a little of what Pete was all about, and gave him a television appearance. I can't remember now what it was, I only know that it led to other appearances, which included Lockett, the chauffeur without a car in the Terry-Thomas show. It was a lovely character, and like all Pete's work, it had gentle humour and pathos. He was a very smart-looking chauffeur with a very smart-looking uniform, but he didn't have a smart-looking car. In fact, he had no car at all. And so he would pretend to drive himself on to the set to pick up his boss, Terry-Thomas. Viewers at that time were inclined to become very involved with the artistes and gradually, as the weeks passed, more and more parts were sent in. First, there was a steering column, then traffic indicators which he attached to his arms, and finally when the series finished he actually drove a complete car onto the set. It was a moment of great triumph, and the viewers loved it. All of these shows were written by Tolly Rothwell and Syd Collins. Tolly by now was becoming more and more successful in his writing.

How sensible Terry was. He realized the value of having strong characters around him, and I never knew him take away a laugh line from anybody. If it was funny, it was good for the show. Later on, in my own television series, one of the writers pointed out that another aritiste would get the laughs in a particular sketch, not me. I felt – like Terry – that it didn't matter as long as it was good for the show. For it's the show your audience remembers.

I became one of Terry's characters, too. Miss Hap, a dizzy secretary, and that's where all my fast songs started from, including the one about the American working-girl, 'Busy, busy'. I sang at great speed:

> *Busy, busy, busy, busy,*
> *All day long I'm in a whirl,*
> *Busy, busy, till I'm dizzy,*
> *Heaven help a working girl.*

I felt I didn't have any particular character, and it quite worried me. Others had funny hairdos and funny glasses. Mine seemed very straightforward. But it developed somehow in its own way, and became very strong.

Another lovely character in the show was that of Rosie Lee, played by Avril Angers, pushing her trolley around the way Sue Pollard does now in *Hi-de-Hi*. Of course, all these shows were live. When you finished a scene you tore up to the other end of the studio for the next one. They didn't have five cameras around then. Leaping over cables and ducking under the camera, you needed to be both a sprinter and an artiste!

Pete was excellent in pantomime. He was a wonderful pantomime dame, warm and sympathetic, and had a great rapport with the children. The outcome of all this was his own television series, *Saturday Special*. Harry Corbett and Sooty started their lives in this programme. Harry with his outraged looks, and 'Oh Sooty, what have you done that for?' when the water-pistol went all over his face. He loved that little puppet. In later years he told me how he and Marjorie, his wife, had gone on a cruise. They were sitting in their cabin before the ship sailed and she said, 'You're not really happy, are you Harry?' 'No, I'm not,' he said, 'I've left Sooty behind.' He couldn't bear it, so he dashed off the ship and brought him back. He said to me, 'I owed such a lot to that little feller, I just had to take him with us.' He and Marjorie (though everybody calls her Tobes – that's her nickname, because she says she looks like a Toby jug) were our great friends, and though we don't see each other now as often as we would like to, when we do meet up all the old warmth is still there.

Rutherglen Main Street, and its famous Town Hall

They gave Chris a car to stop her crying

Just look at that mike!

Private Janet Brown

Me in 'Stars in Battledress', with
my false hairpiece!

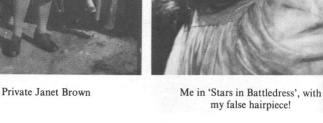

Out of the Forces. Hiding behind the mike is Kemlo Stephens, conductor
of the Scottish Variety Orchestra, while Robert Wilson has – as usual – his thumb
in his belt

Our wedding: Mother on the left, Chris on the right. They say it's lucky when a pigeon 'spots' you – Pete said it was lucky it wasn't an elephant

Pete and I on our honeymoon in Denmark in November, looking very cold-faced

In the window of our cottage in Sussex

My favourite picture of Pete – he always took the ivory tusks off th bonnet, so they couldn't be stole

On stage with Carol Channing at the Palladium

I sent this photo to an old lady, Jean Mackie, in Rutherglen – she wrote, 'The Queen looks pleased to meet you!'

Talking to Prince Charles about impressions

I have Esther's teeth in, but the rest of the outfit is Janet Street-Porter's

My eyebrows are soaped out, and
Marlene's pencilled in

Dolly Parton and all that foam
rubber!

Mrs Thatcher told me she was wearing her Marks and Spencer's outfit that day

Joan said, 'I want this one for the top of my piano!'

With Tyler and Emma.
This photo was taken by David Secombe – Harry's son

Saturday Special alternated with the tremendously popular *Whirligig*, and the focal point of that show was Humphrey Lestoq. I wonder if you remember his phrase 'Goody, goody gumdrops', and the puppet Mr Turnip? Both of these shows were loved by the children.

Freda Lingstrom was head of Children's Television at that time, and she ruled with a very firm hand, always keeping a strict watch on all the material. Everyone knew of Freda's memos that would arrive on their desk either with a reprimand or with a compliment on their work. She was also creator of *Andy Pandy*. We visited her once when our children, Tyler and Emma, were small. She talked about Andy Pandy, but they didn't see him. 'It would spoil the illusion for them, to see him with strings,' she said, and so he remained a star apart.

During this time I was contacted by one of my old Army officers, Donald Wilson, who later produced *The Forsyte Saga*. He was the officer who had taken care of me when we had driven in the jeep in Holland. Out of the blue he phoned to say that a film about the Scottish shipyards was to be made at Pinewood. He was the producer, and he asked me if I would like to do a test for one of the characters in the film.

I'll never forget my first meeting with Donald and the director of the film, Freddy Young, at the Dorchester. It was in the lounge, and we had arranged to meet for tea. I had come straight from rehearsals and I was wearing a lovely new soft, yellow woollen coat. It was the 'New Look', and so it was very long. But underneath was another matter. Suddenly I heard, 'Would you kindly take your coat off and walk to the ladies' room, so that we can get a better idea of your build?'

Oh agony! I knew that under the coat was a faded blue woollen dress, that the side fastening had gone and the hemline was very, very high. What humiliation! I swallowed hard, said very casually, 'Of course,' removed my coat and walked off into the ladies' room. It was Ascot week, and as I walked into the cloakroom I was confronted by elegant women with beautiful dresses nearly to the ground, all wearing beautiful hats and impeccable make-up. In the mirror all I could see was this sad little dress, way above my knees, the bursting seam and a face that registered absolute hopelessness. I swore then that it was definitely the last time I'd ever be caught out over clothes, and I've really tried to keep that resolution. Later I told Donald about my agony over it all, and he said they knew, and they understood, but they·admired me because I managed to carry it through.

Anyway, I was given the part of Rosie in *Floodtide*. It was in this film I first met Gordon Jackson. He was a terrible giggler and it was very difficult to say lines to him without having to stop and start again. Rona Anderson and Elizabeth Sellars were also in the cast. I think it was a first film for everyone.

My boyfriend in the film was Jimmy Logan. I was taken to see Jimmy at the Metropole Theatre in Glasgow. I had never met him before. He was working there with his family, his father, mother and his brother Buddy. In one sketch, I remember, he was dressed as a schoolboy and sat up in the box in a black-out and spot singing 'When I leave this world behind'. You could have heard a pin drop. He had a tremendous personality and was adored by the Scottish audiences.

While filming one day, someone said, 'We're stuck for a line here,' and I suggested a line for one of the scenes: we had a party going, the noise was tremendous. A knock came at the door, and a voice asked, 'Who can that be?', and the line I gave was, 'It'll be the neighbours next door asking for their chairs back.' When I saw the film and heard the audience laugh I was terribly pleased. My first bit of scriptwriting for the movies.

At this stage, Alastair Sim came into my life. Alastair had seen *Floodtide*, and decided I should be Nellie in James Bridie's new play *Mr Gillie*. He wrote asking me to come and see him, this great big man with those enormous penetrating eyes. It's been said that he wasn't all that tall, but to me he certainly was – he towered over me. I must know Bridie's plays? No, I didn't. A look of horror came on Alastair's face. 'Sit down here,' he said, pointing to the sofa. 'Read this, and tell me what you think.' I was given a large tin of biscuits to help myself from, and away I went. I loved the play. And when Alastair asked me what I thought, I discovered all the bits I especially liked were the ones he liked. That settled it. 'When I produce this play, I want you to be my Nellie.' I was elated. My world had been one of Variety, and now I was going to enter a completely different one.

I was earning very good money now in Variety. I certainly wouldn't have as much in the straight theatre, but none of that was important. It was a new challenge, and I wanted to try it. Months went past, and nothing happened. I rang Alastair. Had he changed his mind? 'No, there has just been a delay', but he would definitely be putting it on and I would certainly play the part.

And so I did. There was so much to learn. I loved it. In Variety the essential thing is to get out on the stage and register with your audience within a couple of minutes. You have to make contact directly with your audience. Now here I was, everything completely reversed. I was learning that even if you had nothing to say, your job was to contribute to the scene – you played to each other, not out front, and above all you listened to what was being said to you.

Alastair shook me vigorously by the shoulders one day: 'You're not listening to what I'm saying, girl.' And I was quite surprised. 'Why, no, Alastair, I'm just waiting till you've finished your lines so that I can start mine.' Such a lot to learn!

Alastair was a wonderful teacher, though he could be cruel to be kind. At one rehearsal I had to make an entrance, swinging my handbag. He suddenly stopped me. 'Look, this is what you're doing,' and he minced across the stage – it looked dreadful. 'I don't want a Variety act from you.'

That did it. I felt my eyes fill with tears in my distress at being shown up in front of such fine actors as George Cole and Megs Jenkins – I just wanted to dig a hole for myself. But I knew immediately what he meant, and I saw what I was doing. That one line had said more than a dozen might have done. By the time Alastair had finished working on the scene with me and I finally played it, there was a round of applause every night on my exit. If my family read this, they'll say, 'That's because the audience was glad to see you go!'

Alastair taught me so much, and I'll always be grateful for it. To please him was everything, and the hug he would give me and the delight he would express when things were right were wonderful.

In the play, George Cole played the part of my boyfriend Tom Donnelly, who became my husband. To begin with at rehearsals I found him shy and withdrawn, rarely coming out to lunch with the others. But as we came to know each other more I realized he had a marvellous sense of humour and we laughed a lot together. Oh, how important a good sense of humour is! He gave me endless help and was patient and understanding about my lack of experience, as was everyone else in the cast. Megs was especially kind. She even helped me with the one and only dress I ever made – I was sewing between scenes. She warned, 'You'll never be able to sew properly, doing it like this,' but I was so anxious to wear it and in such a hurry that the pockets fell off the first time I put it on!

It was all so different from backstage in Variety. *There* it was music and noise, but *here* it was a polite knock on the door – 'Your call, Miss Brown'. And carpet backstage, so that when you walked you didn't make any noise. I found the quietness a bit much to take at times, and occasionally had to burst into song in the dressing-room just to break the silence. I took one of my Peggy Lee records in, popped it on my record player, plugged into the wrong voltage and – bang! The electrician said later, looking at the wrecked player, 'It's as if the mice have been in there.'

We opened at the Garrick Theatre, after a short tour including Glasgow. That's where Alastair asked if my mother was at the opening night, and I told him she'd decided to wait till the end of the week when we knew our words better. That floored him, and he laughed that laugh of his – a mixture of delight and disbelief.

When the run finished, Alastair told me he felt very strongly that I should remain an actress. My answer to that was: 'Alastair, you're a star and you can wait to do something you want to. I've got to eat and I must earn, and I can't afford to wait around.' And so I went back into Variety and travelling, and again away from Pete. Always managing to keep going until Thursday – then it was tears, phone calls and a desperate longing to get home. Mondays were travel and band call. Two shows a night. First house, feeling so nervous about how you would fare that it was impossible to eat. Digs were either good or very bad. That awful moment when your taxi drew up in the street where the digs were. 'Oh, I hope the taxi's going to stop here – the curtains look fresh, the path's clean and the brass is shining.' Then the sinking feeling as the cab moved on that extra bit to the one with the grey curtains, the dirty doorstep, and the filthy brass . . . I know we all laugh when we share those moments, but at the time it was far from funny.

Because I was generally the only girl in the show, I had a great deal of time on my own. The other acts were always kind, whether trapeze or conjuring, but the days were so long till the time came to go to the theatre. Tuesday I'd see the town, look at shops. Wednesday, visit the museums, take a run out to nearby beauty spots, if any, but always on my own. By Thursday the tears would flow, and I'd sob my heart out down the telephone. I just longed to finish.

Later on, when I moved up the scale a little more, I stayed at the occasional hotel. There was one in Birmingham in which I had a room that was very, very green. Green carpets, curtains, bedspread and wallpaper. And I remember ringing down for some toast for my breakfast. The incredulous voice at the other end replied: 'If we had to make toast for everyone we'd never get through the day!' After the show, I would come back to the hotel – and there was my table, stark under the one light left on in the dining-room, the usual salad with the plate on top – and the staff gone. I certainly learned what the word 'lonely' meant. But I think deep down in me there is this ability to cope, to take whatever the situation is and try and make the best of it. And I always consoled myself with the thought that everything I did and was experiencing would somehow make the next step easier.

Sundays were taken up with a radio show. So you can see that between travelling and arriving in London, seeing Pete for part of Sunday, then off on Monday again, it was all too much. I wanted to be a good wife too – not just good at my work but also at running a home. Eventually, while playing principal boy in the pantomime *Jack and the Beanstalk* – this time with Pete, at the old Lewisham Hippodrome – I became ill and had to stop work immediately. It was TB and the doctor told me I had to rest as much as possible. I was stunned. To lie in bed when I'd nothing to show for it, not a broken arm or leg – it was very difficult to come to terms with. But the specialist explained that the sooner I rested, the quicker I would be well.

Friends came to see me. They said how tired I looked, how I obviously needed to take it easy, etc. Then the producer of my radio show, Mike Meehan, wrote to me, telling me that he had been in the same situation but worse, and asking if his wife Hope could come and see me. She had, he wrote, a wonderful outlook on life which had helped him get well and he felt sure it would help me. She came to our basement flat in Belgrave Road and she brought so much reassurance and uplift with her. Instead of accepting the obvious picture of me as a sick human being, she saw me as expressing only qualities of God, such as health, strength and joy, and she managed to convey this sense to me. It was a completely different way of thinking, and though much of it puzzled me at the time, I took her thoughts with me to hospital and the convalescent home. They lifted me above loneliness and fear, and through it I found I could help others around me as well. This attitude of mind has stayed with me ever since, and it has helped me through many a rough patch.

When I finally came home, it was to a new home. Pete had found a little house in Portobello Road. It didn't seem wise to return to the damp basement flat, and besides we felt it crazy to see our hard-earned money being paid out and nothing to show for it at the end of the day. We had talked it over and decided that to buy our own place was the right thing to do.

Pete had been looking all the time I was away, and this was what he'd come up with. When I saw the street for the first time, it looked very sad. Friends asked us, 'What on earth made you take that?' 'Well,' I said, 'it won't go down any more, it's got to come up.' And it did. The other thing in its favour was the fact that the price was all we could afford at the time. It was a dear little house, and Pete had been wonderfully imaginative. Our friend, Don Chaffey, now a television director in Los Angeles (his productions include *Charlie's Angels* and *Hotel*) was broke at the time, had no work, and was happy to lend Pete a hand.

Everything, it seemed, had to be right for my homecoming. The house had been painted white, the front door Siamese pink, the walls in the narrow hall were a pink and white candy stripe, and the carpet deep red. It looked terrific. The final touch – and I may tell you it was a very hot day – was our Cairn, Mrs Gillie, sitting panting in front of a coal fire.

I loved our little house, it was so pretty. 'What colours do you want for your kitchen?' 'Oh, I think the colours on the Vim tin.' And so he painted the fireplace blue and lined it with yellow. We had red gingham curtains and a stable door. It was sweet, and we were very happy in it. I was staggered at all the new carpets, chairs, furniture. 'Is it paid for?' I asked anxiously. 'No, but it will be. We'll pay it off as we work.' And we did. I used to hear people say as they passed the house, 'Who lives in there? They must be foreigners to have a door that colour.' We were the first in the road to have a brightly-coloured door.

I had been told to take things easy to begin with, but I was eager to get back to work and delighted when I was offered the part of Dandini in *Cinderella*, at what is now known as the Shaftesbury Theatre – then it was the Princess. The panto-mime was put on by Bertram Montague and the cast included Cherry Lind, Derek Roy and Christine Norden, who played principal boy. My dressing-room was up several flights of stairs, and I can still recall how thrilled I was to run up and down them feeling fit and well again. Our reviews were good. *The Times* wrote: 'Only the Dandini of Miss Janet Brown squares up to the audience with really engaging confidence.' I felt on top of the world.

By the summer of 1952 Pete and I were both involved in children's television – Pete with programmes like *Peter's Travels* and *Butterworth Time*. I had appeared as a guest in most of the evening shows, and following the Terry-Thomas series had gone on to work with Eric Barker and Pearl Hackney in their television programme. Eric was a brilliant satirical writer – how we could do with some of his work now! He both wrote and performed his own sketches, and I played all kinds of parts which I thoroughly enjoyed. By now I had been given my own children's programme, *Toyshop*. It was a nice idea. I had a shop window with all kinds of toys in it, and as the owner of the shop I used to pick up different toys, show them to the children and pretend to sell them. They liked to see the cash register buttons pressed down and the little drawer opening and me handing them imaginary change. The interest lay in the items. If I picked up roller skates, for example, and pretended to hand them over, the cameras would zoom in and the skates would dissolve into a skating act. It was good fun and I began to feel a very real contact with my child viewers. They wrote me lots of letters, and sent me lots of drawings. Children used to come knocking at the door in Portobello Road. They'd come up from the market end. 'Hello, Janet. Can we use your toilet?' And they'd troop upstairs and – after a very long time – troop down again. I think they used to look at the nude paintings in the loo. 'Where's your central heating, Janet?' 'Where's your TV set, Janet?' Our set was so small that it passed unnoticed. They were obviously used to a great many more material comforts than we were. I felt I had gone down a peg or two when I was unable to show them any central heating pipes.

While I was in hospital I'd been offered a film part by Frank Launder, which of course I couldn't accept. But he didn't forget. When another of James Bridie's plays, *It Depends What You Mean*, was adapted for the screen, he rang my agent. The title of the film had been changed to *Folly to be Wise* and Frank wanted me for the part of Jessie, the ATS secretary to

the Army padre, Alastair Sim. Hooray! I was going to work
with Alastair again. And with George Cole.

When I started at Shepperton I met the others in the cast –
among them Elizabeth Allen, Roland Culver, Miles Malleson
and Peter Martyn, who was to play my boyfriend and who
died tragically at a very young age. Above all, there was the
terrifying Martita Hunt. The first day on the set I watched as
she prepared to enter. She took a deep breath, raised her head
high and with nostrils flaring like those of a finely-tuned
racehorse, she descended upon Alastair. They were both so
polite and considerate to each other. 'Am I standing in your
light, darling?' I had no idea you had a light of your own until
the lighting man explained: 'Now, Janet, see that light up
there? When you feel it on you, that's your light, make sure
you get in it.'

After watching Martita's regal entrance, I asked her how
she managed to look as if she was gliding across the set. She
explained. 'The deep breath lifted the diaphragm. Now feel
my rib-cage. Absolutely solid. Hit it, hit it. Now walk on it,
walk like that.' And there was I, me, who had never given a
thought to breathing, suddenly taking great gulps of air, and
trying my best to do it Martita's way. I didn't do it too well,
and decided to settle for the way I'd been before. Though I've
described her as terrifying, she was not to me. It was the
make-up girls – they were afraid to touch her face, and used to
stand shaking in the make-up room before she arrived. 'Don't
use that brush, it's much too hard. Careful with that sponge.'
They were nervous wrecks! I have a vivid memory of her
sitting in her chair between takes, eyes firmly focused on the
racing page. She was a great one for the horses.

Frank Launder was a quiet and gentle director and Alastair
seemed to find it hard to accept his way of directing me. He
would hover behind the set, whispering that I would get much
more out of it if I tried his approach, and that he would 'back
me all the way'. It was confusing at times, but somehow I
think a compromise was reached that pleased them both.

Finding a character isn't an easy job. In *Mr Gillie*, after
trying long and hard to achieve what Alastair wanted from me,

I bumped into James Bridie in the stalls. In desperation I asked, 'What kind of girl is Nellie, what is she really like?' And to my consternation, he replied, 'I'm not sure myself, but what you're doing is just fine.'

After three years of life being very hectic for Pete and me and with the phone always ringing and both of us constantly on the go, there was a kind of restlessness. Whenever we returned to town after being away working, it was 'What film is on at the top of the road?' and 'Let's eat out.' Finally we decided to leave London, and move to the country.

It was our first experience of selling a house. And a very interesting one it was too. We discovered that it is not the people who fall all over you and say how sweet the property is that do anything about it, but the one who is non-committal and hardly shows any interest, is the one who then puts in an offer. Before we left, my mother stayed with us once again. She was very wary of the telephone. I showed her how to dial TIM, the speaking clock. She then dialled, and as the voice said, 'At the third stroke, it will be one forty and thirty seconds,' she said 'Thank you.' And as the voice repeated itself: 'At the third stroke, it will be one forty and forty seconds,' again she said, 'Yes, yes, thank you.' And as the voice started again, she said in desperation, 'Jan, I've said yes, but she won't go away.'

The phone had never stopped ringing in town. Now, in the country, we'd stare at it, saying, 'Is it never going to ring?' Many of the calls had been from song-pluggers, who used to ring up and try and persuade you to sing their song on your next broadcast or television show. There was great competition between music publishers as to whose song could get the most plugs, but just the same, they thought twice before dialling an out-of-town number.

We'd moved to Ifield outside Crawley in Sussex, and had rented a lovely unfurnished house with its own tennis court and orchard. We had forty apple trees. Our friends in town had said they'd give us a year, and then we would have had enough and would be back in London. This is why we thought it wise to rent rather than buy, in case we didn't find it working out.

We had finished furnishing all the rooms but one, a large sitting-room, and one night as we came back after a show we saw that the lights were on all over the place. We dashed in to find that the house had been burgled. Now, the room that had never been furnished had been used to throw all our extra things into, props, old cases, bits of furniture – it was a shambles. When the police arrived to check round and see what damage had been done, they threw open the door to this room and I heard the sergeant say, 'My God, the burglers have made a right mess in here.' Talk about embarrassment!

The year 1954 brought Pete and me together in what I think must have been the first domestic comedy of its kind on television. Written by Syd Collins and Tolly Rothwell and produced by Bill Ward, *Friends and Neighbours* was a series about two young married couples living in adjoining flats. Pete and I played one couple, and Avril Angers and Benny Lee the other. Just as in the Terry-Thomas show, the viewers became involved. They wrote telling us of their own domestic situations which they thought could be included in our script. We had a signature tune for the show – Tolly and Syd wrote the words, Malcolm Lockyer the music. They were so ashamed at how corny the lyrics were that they gave false names. We made a record of it, singing:

> *If you've got friends and neighbours*
> *All the world is a happier place. . . .*

The song went to number one, and you still hear it on the radio.

Although everyone had wished the series luck, the situations in many cases were too far-fetched. And though the artistes and writers learnt a great deal from it, the contract wasn't renewed.

Pete and I didn't see all that much of our house in the country, we always seemed to be dashing off to town. Our cleaning lady said it was like working for ghosts. Nevertheless, neither of us had any desire to live in London again. We had a little flat in town, but loved getting back to the country.

I stood one day in the garden. It was looking lovely – the blossom was on the apple trees and I suddenly thought 'We ought to be sharing this, there should be children to climb those trees and enjoy it all with us. Not just Pete and me wrapped up in what each other is doing. And talking about what funny things the dog has done.' Up till now a career had been the thing. I'd never had any feeling of not being complete. In fact, it irked me when someone would say sympathetically, 'No children? Oh, you're not complete, are you, till you have a family.' I resented this. We'd meant so much to each other. But now I wanted all we were enjoying to be shared.

It's difficult to explain my feelings when I found we were going to have a baby. We wanted this baby, it was no surprise item. But just the same, when I did tell Pete I was pregnant his first words were: 'What on earth will Bob Tronson say?' Robert Tronson was one of our closest friends. He had been in the Navy, but was now a television director; he and Pete shared a great rapport and talked often of the Navy life they had both known before acting days.

'What an extraordinary thing to say!' I looked at Pete in amazement. 'Whenever I've read about situations like this the man is so overcome he can't speak, and has to look out of the window.' For both of us, it was coming to terms with something so far removed from all we had known and shared that it acted on us in a strange way. For me to say the word 'pram' was like speaking a foreign language. Baby shops, and looking at baby clothes, registered little with me. I just felt awkward. I'd find myself saying to Pete, 'We'll have to get, you know, a *thing* for it to lie on, and a *thing* to take it out in . . .'

Though I'd stated very firmly that having a baby wouldn't alter anything for us, I couldn't help thinking, 'Although the baby isn't here yet, it isn't half making its presence felt!' A shelf had to be cleared for nappies, a space for a pram, and so

it went on. There was no doubt 'it' was making its own place
in our home.

For some time we had been looking for a house of our own,
instead of a rented one. I sat reading the descriptions sent by
the estate agents. 'Look, there's one here with its own moat!'
That meant a stream that ran past the door, and generally a
great deal of damp. 'A wealth of old oak beams' turned out to
be just that – but no roof! Each time I was filled with
enthusiasm, and when another cottage was described to us as
'full of character' I wasn't surprised to find out it had been
empty for a year, lacked a dining-room floor, had neither loo
nor electricity and that the roof had holes in it. But when we
saw it we loved it, and decided to buy it.

We'd made up a little song which we used to sing while we
were driving round in the car looking for the place that would
finally be ours. One of the local firms of estate agents were
Taylor, Wood and Gardner, and to the tune of 'The Yellow
Rose of Texas' we sang:

> *Taylor, Wood and Gardner*
> *Are coming just to see*
> *If they can find a house, dear,*
> *A house for you and me*

I know it was crazy, but we got a lot of fun out of it. Now we
wouldn't need to sing it any more.

I was still working, and made my final appearance at the
Pavilion Theatre, Glasgow, in Variety, when I was seven
months pregnant. The baby doll look was all the fashion,
which was just as well for me. The style was almost Empire
line, high-waisted with a very full skirt. I was sewn into my
dress every night because I never knew what size I might be. I
must have looked fairly OK because the first morning I was
standing at the side of the stage as the producer was organizing
the opening of the show. He turned to me and said, 'If you
could do a little tap routine with the girls, that'll look good.' 'I

hardly think so,' I said, removing my loose coat. He hurriedly agreed!

I stayed that week in Rutherglen with my mother, climbing the three flights of stairs to the top flat in the tenement building, the only home I'd ever known in Scotland. Due to the generosity of my mother's neighbours, I'd put on an extra stone. 'Just a wee pancake for Jenny's tea, Mrs Brown.' Or 'A nice bowl of celery soup when she gets back tonight.' They were all so kind. Being good neighbours was the rule rather than the exception, with everyone showing great compassion and understanding if somebody wasn't too well.

When I left for Scotland we were still living at Ifield, and making trips to our new abode each day. It was two farm labourers' cottages knocked into one and the effect was charming. But what a lot of work had to be done! I scraped walls and cleaned floors, Pete mixed cement, without a cement mixer, and in the process thought he was about to leave this world. He told me later he'd written a will, leaving me his Jaguar. He worked miracles, even wiring the house himself. Years later the switchboard went up in smoke due to overloading, and the official from the electricity board said that the whole place could have caught fire, and that it had been very badly done. Of course I said nothing. But as Pete had done it all from library books I still think it was a pretty good effort.

Just as I had returned to Portobello Road and an 'instant' house, so I returned to our cottage in the country to find a log fire burning in the inglenook fireplace, the brass shining and everything looking so welcoming. I was thrilled.

6

Family And Theatre

It was decided that I would have the baby at Redhill, it seemed the sensible thing to do. Pete was going to be in pantomime in Sheffield, and our friends Mike and Joan Ormond who lived at Godstone, and with whom we had often stayed, kindly said I could be with them. It was only a short distance to the maternity home.

Life with the Ormonds was never quiet. There were five young children – when they heard I had to watch my weight and stick to a strict diet, they took great delight in coming into my bedroom, standing round the bed and holding a box of chocolates. 'Come on, Jan,' they'd coax, 'have one, just one.' There was also a parrot, named Henry, who gave me the fright of my life when he burst into song. I think he must have been frightened by an opera singer. 'La la la la, la la la la,' he'd warble, followed by a screech and the command, 'Go to bed, go to bed.' Henry was quite a character.

The baby arrived in February, right on time. It was a boy – the matron came bustling in asking for a matinée jacket to put on him. All I had was a bit of knitting still on the pins – it looked more like tripe. She was disgusted with me. 'Mrs Butterworth, you had nine months to get all this together.'

'Ah, yes,' I said, 'but I didn't know who it was for.' Somehow the whole thing had been so unreal for me. Now it was a different story. I looked at this little thing in my arms. He was beautiful. Not all wrinkly like a walnut, but beautiful. And I was completely overwhelmed. Such small fingers and tiny nails. No one could have been more surprised than I was at the strength of my feelings. In a way it was like falling in love all over again. My matter-of-fact attitude had completely flown out of the window. Now I found myself looking at skies and stars with completely new eyes. Everything was so beautiful. Even the poems I read in *Country Life* were beautiful! I was never any good at visualizing, but now – oh, now I knew what I'd got.

Pete motored down from Sheffield just to be with me for a short while on the Sunday, and to see his new son. He was shattered by it all as well. Poor Pete! He wanted to talk, but was so tired he fell asleep in the chair. Later on he phoned from Sheffield, and we discussed names. 'How about calling him Michael, after Mike Ormond?' 'Oh that's a lovely idea.' Then another call: 'Everyone says, 'How's young Pete getting on?' 'All right,' I said, 'let's have Michael Peter Butterworth.'

Long after the baby had been registered in that name, Pete announced, 'I feel any name attached to Butterworth is going to sound like a comedian. I think he should have the name Tyler.' By this time I honestly didn't care. 'Fine,' I said, and promptly added the extra name on, having to go back to the office and pay an additional sum for the new title. Pete's explanation of all this was: 'When people hear the name Tyler they'll say "That's an interesting name", and forget the funny one, Butterworth.' And how right he was!

One day I saw a big van go through the town, and written on the side in large letters was 'Tyler of Tonbridge'. Great, I thought, it sounds just like 'Montgomery of Alamein'. I was told later it was a shoe shop!

I remember him at a very young age playing with another family on the beach. When I went over to collect him the woman looked at me. 'I've been asking the little boy what his name is, and he says it's Caravan.'

'Oh no,' I laughed, 'his name is Tyler.'

'Poor little thing,' she said, 'no wonder he calls himself Caravan.'

But back to the baby days. I read up all the articles in magazines – 'It is important to have a play time with your child.' Yes, yes, how right they were, and the baby who had been perfectly happy up till then would be taken from his cot, placed on the floor for mother and child to have a precious moment together. But the baby, who hadn't read the article and wasn't in on all this play time routine, created hell! I quickly decided we had better just go on in our own way and enjoy each other's company when we felt like it!

Peter was as bad as I was and had gone quite into reverse with his attitude towards babies. He adored our son, and was deeply sentimental about everything to do with him. In later years Tyler's rattle still hung by the side of the fireplace and his first shoes were still in a box in the loft.

When Tyler was four months old, Pete and I went to Edinburgh to play a summer season together, the first since our starting days at Scarborough. It was the Lyceum Theatre and the show was Howard and Wyndham's *Half Past Eight*. Dickie Hurron was the producer. As I had wanted to continue with work, and Pete was very keen that I should, we found ourselves a nanny – a wonderful girl, Doris Jackson, who came from Yorkshire. A no-nonsense girl, willing but without any training. This was tricky, and we went through several difficult periods. 'I won't have to wear a uniform, will I?' she said aggressively. 'Of course not, just as you are is fine.' 'Just as you are' meant a petunia-coloured woollen dress which clashed badly with her red hair. It was only when we got to know each other better that I discovered it was her *only* dress.

Anyway, here we all were in Edinburgh, with a cast we'd never met before, and a theatre we had never played in – it was all very exciting. We found temporary accommodation, but we really needed a house for the season. I enjoyed going to estate agents to see what they might come up with. I always had a feeling that there must be a right place for us, even when the girl looked through the books saying, 'No, sorry, nothing.' It's the expectancy and the lovely surprise and feeling of gratitude when you've been taken care of.

Our house was in Craiglockhart on the outskirts of the town. In the evenings you could hear the bagpipes in the distance. I think that's the best way to hear pipes – in the distance. They were practising for the Edinburgh Tattoo. It was a great house, and when we came to know the cast better

we had some wonderful parties there after the show at night.
They would go on till the dawn came up and the birds were
singing. Happy, happy times.

Some of the people in that *Half Past Eight Show* were
Scottish comedian Rickie Fulton – how the Edinburgh
audiences loved him – Digby Wolfe, known to the London
audiences but like us appearing for the first time in a Scottish
review; and Jean Bayliss, a beautiful red-haired singer. Jean
and her husband David were to become among our closest
friends, and that friendship is as strong now as it was then.
Jean's son, Daniel, was six months old when we all met up,
two months older then Tyler. But the big difference was that
he had a trained nanny. Nanny Elizabeth had gone through a
very rigorous training in Aberdeen, but – and it's a very big
but – when she and Doris met up they became firm friends,
and like Jean and I have remained so throughout the years.
Elizabeth, seeing that all wasn't well, took Doris to one side
one day and said in her lovely Aberdonian accent, 'I'm going
to give you some classes, otherwise you'll not be staying with
the Butterworths.' She did just that, and Doris – eager to learn
the right way – was a quick pupil. How to bath the baby
properly, put him to bed, feed him etc. – all were gone into,
the two of them enjoying sharing each other's company,
especially as my days, and Pete's, were taken up with
rehearsals from nine-thirty in the morning, and then there
were the shows at night. It was heavy, and we were dead beat
at times, but we loved it.

One day Doris came to me. 'Can I wear a uniform?'
Elizabeth always wore hers; with its starched white collar and
little white puff armlets on the sleeves, it looked good. I was
astonished, knowing how she had felt about such things. 'Why
a uniform, Doris?' 'Oh, because everybody looks at you in
Woolworth's, and they stop the traffic in Princes Street when
you want to take the pram across the road.' I didn't mind at
all, and what it did for Doris was remarkable. Somehow the
uniform gave her the identification she needed – she knew her
job now, knew what she was, and she was filled with pride.
She went home to see her parents, came back to us in her

uniform of green looking marvellous, and from then on not only was Tyler taken care of, but Pete and I were as well. She was tremendous – such authority. So much so, that one day when all the company set off on a steamer to see some of the glorious scenery on the west coast and a man on the boat fainted, Doris was immediately asked what should be done. She said, in her best nurse's voice, 'Loosen his collar', then smartly disappeared.

She loved Tyler, and stayed with us for several years. Where we would have been without Nanny Doris, I hate to think. When she finally left us to be married, it was hard to reconcile the girl who had arrived in that petunia dress with the girl giving a farewell party in the cottage to all the friends she had made during her years with us. Mr and Mrs B. thought the world of her, and missed her very much when she had gone. Tyler, too, for a long time, felt the gap.

The show was excellent experience. I did my own spot, which included impressions of Eartha Kitt, Joyce Grenfell, Lena Horne, and then there were sketches, playing different characters. Some of the material came from West End reviews. I remember singing a clever song called 'Little Black Dress' by Ronnie Cass and Alex Grahame. The singer wore a basic black dress, to which she could add any number of things – a scarf, bag, and so on to make it look chic. In the end it was covered with bits and looked a right old mess! All the props were arranged on what looked like a large set of railings, each item carefully hung over or placed against it. I stood ready behind the curtains one evening waiting for my music to start, and as the drapes went back one caught the umbrella and sent it flying to the floor. Oh lor, I thought, now what. The song was such a fast one, and everything had to be picked up and put on so quickly. I started off happily enough:

> *A little black dress that you can wear*
> *To each and every function,*
> *A little black dress of savoir faire*
> *From here to Clapham Junction . . .*

I moved to the scarf, then on to the hat, all the time aware that the umbrella was lying further downstage. And then I did the fatal thing – as I approached it my concentration went, and so did my words. I didn't want to stop, I felt sure they would come back, and so I continued:

> *A little black dress that you can wear*
> *A little black, black dress*
> *A little black dress that you can wear*
> *A black, black, black, black dress . . .*

I could see the audience's faces looking decidedly bewildered, but I still didn't give up. Moving to the edge of the stage I looked down into the pit and into the face of the pianist who was looking up at me.

> *Do you know the wo-ords . . .?*

I sang. His flat-footed 'No' made me stop. I apologized to the audience and explained what I had done. I then said, if they didn't mind, I would go back to the top, right to the beginning again . . . and that's what I did. That night they got two renderings for the price of one!

Having the baby had altered things. I had said it wouldn't, but as far as work was concerned it certainly did. I still played in shows, but they became fewer. I appeared in pantomime in Sheffield, and Tyler had his first birthday party there. Gradually managements and agents started to say I probably didn't want to bother working – after all I had a husband who was now becoming more and more successful, and somehow, apart from anything else, the children's television programmes had moved me into another category. I was now being called 'Aunt Janet' which I didn't like one bit. Offers for evening television shows completely faded out. Apart from a lunchtime programme from Birmingham – I think it was called *Rainbow Room* – when I proudly sang 'It's a boy, It's a boy' after having Tyler, and the odd appearance on television, everything more or less had come to a halt. I longed to be wanted by a management, to be needed by someone.

Then suddenly, right out of the blue, I heard from Alastair Sim again. He was going to do a play called *The Bargain* written by Michael Gilbert, and would I go and see him? Again I went off full of excitement. There was Alastair. There was George Cole. I came away walking on air. We were all going to work together once more. Alastair loved to keep people around him that he liked, and I was over the moon at the thought of doing the play and being back with friends. Again, Alastair had cast me as an empty-headed tartish girlfriend to George. Was there a message here? Actually, it was all in such contrast to my own straight way of behaving, and I noticed as rehearsals went on how Alastair was making me feel younger and more flippant. The difficult part for me was the sexy side of it. George came to me at rehearsal one afternoon: 'I think it would help if you shortened your skirt – you know, pull it up a bit.' I was very wary about this and hesitantly pulled it up, only to surreptitiously pull it down again when I thought no one was looking. But it didn't fool Alastair. I had to make my skirts shorter. They pointed out I had nice legs. I had no idea I had.

Before the next rehearsal, Alastair and George must have had other discussions, this time about my top. I'm not what you'd call generously endowed.

'Could you,' George quietly and very embarrassedly said, 'sort of . . . inflate them?' I blushed furiously as always, and went out and bought a padded bra. Oh the humiliation, when later in the day George came over to me. 'I'm sorry to go on about all this but could you possibly . . .?' 'But I've done it,' I said.

Finally I arrived at a figure that pleased them, and must have looked the part, for one bitchy lady was later heard to say grudgingly that I was 'very good, but then you can see it's type-casting.'

Apart from being George's girlfriend in the play, I was also Alastair's secretary. During one performance I made my usual entrance, stood by his desk to take notes and realized I'd forgotten my pad. I nearly died, I had my little extra lines written on the pad. 'Er, excuse me, sir,' I made up the lines, 'I've just left something in the outer office. May I go and get it?' His huge eyes looked at me, the tongue slid round the lips. 'No, certainly not.' Afterwards I said to him, 'That was a bit mean Alastair, why didn't you let me go?' Again the look. 'What was I supposed to be doing while you were off?' A very good point.

I was learning. But my first experience with Mr Gillie had taught me a good deal: I was now no longer a newcomer to the legitimate stage. It was as lovely as ever to be working with Alastair, and after a short tour we came in to the St Martin's Theatre. The play wasn't a great success, but it ran for several months. I felt strangely sad when it finished. It had been a happy cast with George Cole, Peter Copley and Helen Christie, and we had shared lots of good times on tour. Now it was over. Usually I can't wait to clear my dressing-room when a production is coming to an end. I used to wonder at dancers in pantomime crying as they left the theatre, for once I knew it was only a week or so till the show finished, I was impatient for what was going to be next. Whether something was actually lined up or not I was keen to move on. So the gingham cloth that covered the dressing-table, the first-night cards, the make-up, all were packed as soon as possible on the last night. A quick dash round with a tissue to remove the scattered talc on the dressing-table and away. Finishing this play was different. It was the end of a happy period, a parting with friends, and I understood why girls cried at the and of a show.

I feel I must mention again how much Alastair taught me. His ability to make a scene fresh each time he did it – this was especially noticeable when the situation was a comedy one. I recollect from filming with him the laughs he got in the scenes. But if he was asked to do another take, he didn't repeat the gestures, he found a fresh approach. His lines, too, were always said as if just coming to mind, not dialogue that had been well rehearsed. It was this apparent searching for words that to me always made the dialogue so natural and real.

Shortly after the play closed, I became pregnant again. Pete and I had discussed how right it would be to have another child – company for Tyler and so on. If the first one was kept fairly secret, this one certainly was not. As soon as I told Pete, he couldn't wait to tell everyone, he was thrilled. Actually I was a bit cross; my pleasure was in keeping the secret as long as possible. Being able to say, 'I'm having a baby, you know,' and the incredulous 'You're not!'

Once more I marched round the lanes, and as the day grew nearer for the newcomer to arrive, so I became more adamant that it must arrive on the day, not one day early, not one day late, but *on the day*. But the baby had a mind of its own and its own idea when it would arrive. 'Go and take a walk round, Mrs Butterworth.' So I walked, jumped – and finally, on the 22nd December, my daughter decided to arrive. 'She won't be here till morning,' said the doctor confidently after examining me about 7 pm. But again this child had other ideas, and arrived smartly late that evening.

I was in the same little maternity annexe in Redhill. It was Christmas and the Salvation Army played carols outside. Pete appeared with all sorts of gifts, amongst them a little tree, all sparkling with lights, that sat on the window ledge. He even pinned an outrageous pair of frilly knickers to the window. All through our marriage, as friends will testify, my expression of 'Oh Pete!' said in shocked tones was frequently to be heard over some outrageous thing he'd done.

We were both so happy. Tyler now had a sister.

Of course we went through all the business of names again.

'How about Caroline?'

'No,' I said, 'I think not.'

'Victoria?'

An uncertain 'yes' from me. And then I said it out loud. 'Victoria Butterworth. No, no good, it sounds like a sponge cake.'

Finally, as with Tyler's name, I gave up. And when Pete rang me to say, 'I think Emma would be lovely,' I responded with relief, 'Oh yes, so do I.'

Then another thought struck him. 'Perhaps she might not

like Emma in later years. Shall we give her another name as well?'

'Okay.'

'Right,' he said, 'my Aunt Suzie was a great character.'

'All right,' again from me. 'Suzie can be her middle name.'

'Spelt S-U-Z-I-E. Not S.'

Later on Emma said to me, 'I can hardly say that to people every time – my name is spelt with a Z not an S.' As I write this it's growing more like Liza Minelli's song: 'Liza with a Zee, not Lisa with an S . . .'

At this point I felt I too must have a share in things.

'My mother's middle name is Russell – that should be there as well.'

So – Emma Suzie Russell Butterworth, poor girl, was launched into the world.

When Tyler was born there were many pictures in the papers, whereas when Emma arrived there was a newspaper strike. It was the weekend, Christmas, and shops shut. Later I had notes from friends: 'You would choose to do this when we can't get any flowers to you.'

I don't know much about post-natal depression. I do know that there was a period of confusion for me whenever I had to make a decision of any kind.

'Stamps, please.'

'What price?' Oh dear, a decision.

Plug for the electric fire. 'What kind?' Another decision. I was quite lost for a while, and in the end made myself say something positive, for right or wrong.

If Pete was thrilled at having a son, he was even more thrilled at having a daughter. He had to make journeys to reach us at the cottage in dreadful weather, only managing to make his way back to Nottingham, where he was playing pantomime, before the snows closed Ashdown Forest and no one could get through.

Tyler loved his new sister. He had been filled with excitement waiting for her, but he hadn't realized that she wouldn't be able to talk or walk right away – that she'd just lie there. This disappointed him beyond measure. Outwardly he was loving, his arm around his baby sister and his little hand holding hers. We discovered later he was actually quietly disjointing her fingers, crushing them as he smiled for the photographers. We had tried to make sure there would be no fuss over the new baby and that he would not be left out of things. But adults have an unconscious way of making this happen: 'What about your new sister, isn't she lovely?'

And there he would stand, politely smiling, while they cooed and clucked and held his sister in their arms. One day, still smiling politely while sitting next to her on the bed, he took a framed picture and bashed her over the head with it. When she was older I could sympathize, as she ruthlessly went about breaking his toys. I think I would have bashed her over the head too!

To make Tyler feel special, we bought a Cairn puppy for him as a companion. She immediately lay outside the door, her little face pressed between her paws as if she knew instinctively what her job was. They became the greatest of friends and were inseparable.

Tolly Rothwell and his wife Scottie came to see us one afternoon. Tolly by now was writing more and more *Carry On* films, and the four of us hadn't seen each other for some time. I am inclined to play things down a bit, and when Scottie came downstairs after leaving her coat in the bedroom she said, 'There's a baby lying on your bed, are you looking after it for a neighbour?'

'No,' I said, 'it's mine.'

She was amazed and quite angry. 'Why didn't you tell me? I would never have come to see you without something for the new baby.' I was made to feel quite bad about it.

Life with Tyler and Emma was pretty full. Doris had got herself engaged to a soldier and was going to live abroad and we had to find another nanny. We had some fun with nannies. The next one, Gillian, was so glamorous that my friend Jean Bayliss, who was visiting us with her husband David, took me into the kitchen one day and asked, 'Have you looked at her?'

'Well, no not really.'

'But haven't you noticed her figure?'

'No,' I said, 'she had her coat on.' All I cared about was finding someone capable.

'Well,' said Jean in a hard tone, 'I wouldn't have her in my house.'

David meanwhile, tried to find excuses to go upstairs and help Nanny with the children's games. Actually, she was a splendid nanny, but she also left to get married.

And then we had Valerie, from Yorkshire. Yorkshire people take some understanding. I found it difficult at times to get the hang of it.

'It's a lovely day, Valerie, would you like to take time off, pop down to Brighton?'

A non-committal 'Don't mind.' Not 'Oh, that would be lovely', or 'Yes, thank you'.

But when I did get the hang of it, and lines like 'Are there any more pots to wash?' – me thinking pots meant saucepans, wondering why on earth having just had a cup of tea we should need to be looking for pots to wash, and her meaning cups and mugs – when all that was sorted out we got on like a house on fire. She was another great girl too. Tyler and Emma called her 'Old Stricty'. She was certainly not old, but strict – yes.

As time went along, things became more difficult for me. I faded more and more into the background. One night, Pete and I went with two close friends, Helen and Jerry Wise, to a fairground and were standing by the shooting range.

''Allo, Pete, all right then?' the man called out as he handed him a gun. 'What about that girl you used to work with, Janet Brown or something? What happened to her?'

What happened, indeed! I could laugh, but I felt deeply the separation from work and more and more the lack of an identity. Never more so than the time we went to the Ideal Home Exhibition where Peter was to open a stall. I stood by the side, and as I reached to try a piece of the cake that was set out on plates I was unceremoniously pushed away: 'Stand back there, lady, Peter Butterworth is about to open this stall.'

I don't think it can ever be easy for two people who share

theatre life if one is a great success and the other is not. No
matter how pleased you are at the other's success, the need to
know that you too are wanted is very strong. Funnily enough,
with us it was a sort of see-saw. When things had been good
for me at the start, they had been tough for Pete. Now the
positions were reversed. I think he was much better about it
than I was. Nevertheless, I tried to keep a philosophical
outlook, and it was pointed out to me once by a friend that I
was where I was most needed, and that when the right time
came for me it would be so much better than I could have ever
thought. And it did turn out that way eventually. But there
was a long way to go.

Being needed meant school runs, sports days, gymkhanas –
I never knew I would feel so competitive about my daughter
winning a race. But I was in there, tearing up and down the
field with her and the pony and willing her to win.

Occasionally I would do a cabaret, but they were few and far
between. And by the time I had finished with pianist and
petrol, I was lucky to have two pounds left. No matter – it was
great just to keep the wheels oiled.

Pete was marvellous with people, he had such ease. Even
when things had been difficult for him he had seemed to be
able to keep this easy charm. I was hopeless. Standing in the
BBC Club, the perspiration making my hands wet, I'd dive off
into the ladies' room – anything rather than feel I looked as if I
were trying to get a job. I found it terribly difficult. Then,
gradually, as I thought through things, I began to see it wasn't
a question of trying to 'get' something, but rather what I had
to give, and so I found myself able to pick up a phone and say
hello to people just because I knew and liked them, not for
what I'd get out of it. This change of attitude was a great help,
and one day I was asked if I would like to go to Lowestoft in a
summer show. Someone had dropped out at the last minute. It
would only be for eight weeks and there was very little money
in it. I didn't care, it was an opportunity and I gladly said yes.

The Rockin' Berries, with Clive Lee, topped the bill. They
were a great act. Clive did some very funny impressions,
including the Singing Postman who was highly popular at that

time, and I did mine. Audiences don't seem to mind lots of impressions, and it didn't create any difficulties for us.

Throughout everything, we tried to keep the family together. The same old problem arose in Lowestoft: 'No houses this late on in the year, all places have been let.' But I had learnt not to accept this picture, and sure enough we ended up with a marvellous little house out near Beccles. Tyler and Emma loved it. Friends came up and enjoyed it with us, and a good time was had by all.

In the past I had appeared in Sunday concerts at the Butlin's holiday camps, and when they offered me a nice long summer contract, I was delighted. The season was at Minehead, but apart from the shows during the week your contract also stipulated that you appear on Sundays at the other camps. This could mean very long car journeys, usually with no one to share them. I did plenty of these, singing and whistling through the night – anything to keep myself awake – usually arriving back at Sussex or wherever absolutely exhausted. In the Brighton Butlin's, which was really a hotel, there was a large sign which intrigued me: 'Do not walk across the ballroom with wet feet'. Afterwards I discovered it was because the swimming pool was nearby.

I worked with lots of fine artistes. Doreen Lavender was one, a sweet singer who held a tiny white poodle in her arms that sang with her. It would throw its little head back and the most mournful 'Ooowls' would come out. And then there was Cliff Henry, a lovely comedian with that look so many comedians have of being funny but with a pathos about them as well. He was a great favourite with the holiday audiences. We did several sketches together, and when we talk now about the laughs we used to have, he'll say, 'I do wish you would do more of the characters you used to do then.' The drunken lady pianist, the jerky early-days-of-the-silent-films actress – I'd forgotten all about them till he reminded me.

After the show we would go to each other's flats. 'What have you brought?' 'Oh, I've got lovely cheese here, what about you?' 'Baked beans.' And then we would cover the table with our food. Everyone would sit around and talk and laugh – that's the wonderful thing about theatre people (here I am saying it again), their sense of humour – and this would go on well into the night.

The shows at Butlin's were great experience. The production was looked after by Dandy Page and Chesney Allen was the agent for them. The stages are enormous in Butlin's. I think the one at Bognor is larger than the Palladium, and the auditorium holds around 3,000 people or more.

In 1966, the year England's football team won the World Cup, I was again appearing at Butlin's – this time it was Bognor. Although I worked at the camp I didn't stay in it, but had a small flat in the town. The day of the final I was glued to the television set. Tyler and Emma were watching with me. The match was against Germany, and what a match it was. We had reached injury time; our players had their socks pulled down around their ankles, their legs were being massaged, and the tears were pouring down my face. 'Come on, come on!' Tyler and Emma looked at me with great anxiety: 'Why are you crying, Mummy?' 'Because we're winning,' I sobbed, 'now eat up your scones and jam.' And they burst into tears as well. I'll never forget that day and the feelings it kindled in me. The players were magnificent. I went to the theatre that night worn out – you'd have thought I'd played in the match myself.

After the Butlin's season I appeared in cabaret aboard the *QE2*. When the ship called in at Piraeus, the port of Athens, I stood leaning against the deck rail fascinated by the busy scene that was taking place before me. I felt I must go ashore. I'd heard from other passengers that it wasn't very wise to go on your own, but I didn't know anyone and I didn't want to be in such a wonderful spot and not see everything. I needed Greek money, and hadn't done anything about getting any changed on the ship, so as soon as I got ashore I made straight for the bank.

Now, for some unknown reason, I wanted to find a doorknob for the cottage. Can you imagine it, a doorknob from Greece! And while trying to explain this to the bank clerk, and not being able to speak the language, I heard a voice at my elbow whisper, 'Can I help you? I am happy to speak the English. It is good practice for me.' A pleasant-looking Greek boy was standing there.

'Oh yes,' I said with great relief, 'I'm just changing some money, and then I want to find a brass doorknob.'

'Ah, you will want Mikanos Square, come – I will show you.'

'Oh, thank you so much.'

He had a friend with him, but somewhere along the way he vanished. We hurried along busy streets, jumped on and off buses, till finally we arrived at our destination. 'Now see,' he said proudly, 'here are your antique stalls. Here you will find doorknobs.' I scurried up and down the lines of stalls, fascinated by all the bits and pieces.

I've always loved wandering around finding bargains. Eventually I found what I wanted. By this time it was lunchtime, and very hot. Out of politeness I offered to buy him a drink and something to eat. I had enormous sunglasses on. He leaned across the table. 'How old are you?' he breathed, 'twenty-seven or twenty-eight?' Oh, dear, what now?

'Er, twenty-seven.'

His eyes gazed into mine, and through my dark glasses I stared out at him. 'I love you,' he suddenly said.

'Oh no,' I told him, 'you can't *love* me, that's the wrong word, we've only just met.' But no, he wouldn't have it. So hurriedly, I thanked him for his help and rose from the table saying my goodbyes. But all wasn't over yet. I was so naive. We went out into the square. By now it was very, very hot indeed. My dark glasses were fixed firmly on my nose. For better or worse they had to stay there. I'd said I was twenty-seven, and the only way to avoid discovery was to keep them on.

'Goodbye,' I extended my hand to shake his.

'Yes, yes, but first we go to hotel and rest.'

'Rest?' I said cheerfully. 'But I feel great. I don't want to rest. In fact, I'm going to climb that hill over there, and visit the church on the top.'

'Yes, yes, but first we go to hotel.'

'Oh,' I said with surprise and relief at understanding him. 'You mean, do I want to go to the ladies' room? No, thank you, no.'

This brought forth, 'Are you being funny, woman?'

I looked at him in bewilderment. The square was packed with passengers from the ship. They kept passing in front of me. 'How do you mean?'

'I speak plainly,' he said. 'I wish to go to hotel room and have intercourse with you.'

Oh dear, heavens! Had anyone from the ship heard the words? My hand flew to my mouth. Goodness, this was awful! I glanced hurriedly around – oh, I hoped no one had heard. I'd be branded as a wicked woman. I heard myself saying, 'I speak plainly. I don't want to go to a hotel room,' and then, 'Was that what was in your mind when you spoke to me in the bank? Well, I'm so sorry, but I've wasted your Saturday. You'll have to find someone else.'

I'll say this for the Greeks, they don't give up easily. And this one stayed with me till I returned to the dock and went up the gangway. 'Now,' I said as I shook his hand firmly, 'I shake hands with you and thank you for a nice day. That's how we do it in England.' He had a dazed look on his face as I waved my farewells and disappeared into the ship.

The American ladies couldn't wait to hear my story. 'My dear, is it true that you were accosted by a Greek?'

Pete's comment when I came home and told him of my adventure was, 'How did you describe a doorknob to him?' The rest is best left unsaid. Only that we laughed a lot about it. The doorknob from Greece is still on the cottage door. I could have bought the same one in Brighton.

7

'Who Do You Do?'

When I returned to London, a new television show called *Who Do You Do?* was on the screen. One of the writers connected with this programme was Dick Vosburgh. I had known Dick from earlier days when he had written commercials for Pete and me. He suggested me to the producer of the programme, Jon Scoffield. I was given a spot in the final show of the first series. By then I had added several more new characters to my list: Cilla Black, Goldie Hawn and Granmaw from the Beverly Hill Billies. Jon was very clever; he had directed my piece with great flair, cutting all the dead wood out and putting on the screen the best of my material. The style of the programme was mainly close-ups against a stark white background, cutting away from one impression to another with great speed. That was its success – the speed of it. No impression lasted long, and that to me is really the way to get the best out of an impression. If you go on too long the illusion disappears. Jon presented me in the best possible light, and the next morning – literally as quickly as that – I was back in business. The phone was ringing, I was being asked to do cabarets and shows – oh, it was wonderful.

I sometimes think of that long spell of practically nothing – the hurt that I'd feel when a producer would say, without meaning to hurt, 'Well, we'll try and find a line for you somewhere,' and the continual walking in Pete's shadow, the longing I felt to do something. With housework I always had this sense that I was doing it before catching a train to get on with my real job – except that there wasn't a train. People have often asked me whether it is easy when you're married and in

112

show business to keep your marriage working. It isn't easy, there has to be a tremendous effort on both sides. We made ridiculous trips just to see each other for lunch. Once I set out in the middle of a snowstorm to get to Pete in Oxford, where he was playing panto. The weather was dreadful and on a hill my car slid straight into a hedge. A milkman came along, towed me out of the snow and I set off again. When I reached the outskirts of Oxford, what should be coming round the roundabout but the Jag, and Pete.

'Fancy coming out to meet me – how lovely!'

'Meet you?' said Pete, 'I haven't even been to the digs yet.' He'd been stranded on the road all night.

Getting together could be difficult, particularly when I'd been away working. You may recall I explained earlier on that you have to organize everything for yourself. Who was this man telling me I should do this and that? And he, in turn, thinking – who is this woman chattering on so relentlessly? But we could talk about it and sort it out: I sometimes wonder what it's like for, say, a naval wife, whose husband is away for such long spells, and the readjustment that has to be made when they meet up again. Both of you have to try very hard, and Pete and I did. We always shared this great interest in each other's work, and phoned each other every day when we were apart. Pete loved Tyler and Emma so much, hated being parted from them and suffered terrible pangs of homesickness and a need for them when he saw other children playing; he longed to be with his own and he never came home without some special toy or book for them. There was always some surprise tucked away in our cases and great excitement on our return. I remember talking to Harry Secombe about these homecomings. He knew exactly what I meant and told me of one of the times when he returned to his family. 'I walked up the path with my suitcase,' he said, 'and there was Myra and the kids. I was given a great hug and then I walked back down the path to collect the other suitcase in the taxi – my daughter thought I was leaving again, and burst into tears.'

Another question I have been asked is how children feel if their parents aren't with them all the time. I believed, providing the children had their security, and that security wasn't threatened, then all would be well. Doris, our nanny, was there and loved them – really loved them. We knew this and accepted it.

The times when we were all together were marvellous. I recall a pantomime Pete was appearing in at Torquay – as usual we were all going to meet up for Christmas, and I packed the car to the roof. Everything went in, for the flat he had rented didn't sound as if it had much in the way of kitchen utensils and such like. Knives, forks, pans, plates, carving knives, serving dishes – I loaded and loaded.

'Now careful with this, it's a bottle of whisky for Pete's aunt.' Just as we got to the door, it slipped out of my hands and crashed on the steps. The smell of whisky was everywhere. And at that moment Mrs Scott, who kept the house straight for us, came cycling along the road past the postman. As she reached us she snorted, 'Disgusting! Fancy drinking at this hour. You could smell the whisky off him a mile away.'

That particular Christmas was a great success. Not only because we were all together, but because Pete's aunt and cousin were able to share it with us too. I was rather pleased with myself for cooking the turkey and all the trimmings in a strange kitchen and on a cooker I'd never seen before. Isn't it a lovely feeling when everyone raises their glasses to you at the end of the meal and says, 'Congratulations to the cook – a marvellous meal'? Such satisfaction!

When the next series of *Who Do You Do?* came along, I was contracted to appear in it, not just for one programme but for several. I was now performing in sketches with Freddie Starr. What a character – with his blonde hair, piercing blue eyes, and a stammer that would suddenly emerge if he was uneasy or unsure about something! We got on marvellously well together. I was helpless at some of the jokes he played; outrageous, I know, but wonderfully funny. One girl came to the studio to do her act for the first time; she was naturally very nervous with the strangeness of everything and the general air of chaos. She took up her position in the bright studio lighting, the cameras and the crew all around, and began to sing – Freddie suddenly appeared in a raincoat, stood in front of her and gave her a quick 'flash'. He'd nothing on underneath. The song faded in the girl's throat. 'It's no good,' said Freddie, 'I can't work with a girl who forgets her words.'

Preposterous, yes, but oh, how I laughed!

After the television series we did several stage shows together, appearing first at the North Pier, Blackpool, where 'House Full' notices went up throughout the entire run. Later we did the spring show at the Coventry Theatre, and a summer show at the ABC in Yarmouth. Working with Freddie made me change my own act a great deal. Observing how sharp he was on stage, I realized how dated my own presentation and music were, and I made sure that by the time the Coventry show came along I'd changed things considerably, shortening impressions, adding new ones and having fresh orchestrations done.

When the show ended, I said, 'Freddie, I've known some extraordinary moments working with you, and things will never be the same in the theatre for me again. But I'll tell you one thing – life with you is never dull.' When he chose to be, he was absolutely brilliant.

The next television series was called *Now Who Do You Do?* By this time I was in nearly all the programmes, the only resident woman in the show. The others in the team were Paul Melba, Peter Goodright, Roger Kitter, Johnny Moore, and later Little and Large. For many of us, this show was a springboard to even better things.

It was now 1975, and the name Margaret Thatcher was on people's lips. I had seen her on television when she was Minister for Education. I remember especially an interview with schoolchildren, and her reply when they asked if she would like to be Prime Minister. 'Oh, I don't think that will happen in my time.' I was fascinated by her – the low, slow voice, the never-ending sentences, just straight the way through from A to Z. Do I admire her? Yes, I do, enormously. It must take a tremendous amount of courage to throw your hat into the ring, and be prepared to have a go, as she did. Just think of it for a moment: in a man's world, where nothing of this kind had ever taken place before. To everyone's amazement she won the ballot and became Leader of the Opposition.

And the day she won that ballot was the day that changed my career. I was at home in my cottage in Sussex when the phone rang. I picked up the receiver, and a voice at the other end said, 'It's the *Today* programme here.' (This was Eamonn Andrews' topical early evening show.) 'Could you come up to the studios and do a good impersonation of Mrs Thatcher? She's just won the first ballot.'

A good impersonation? I was just about to say, 'I'm sorry, but I can't do one of her,' when the thought came, well why not? I don't know of anybody else who does it – and to my surprise I heard myself saying, 'Yes.' Then I asked, 'But what about the script?' I was told that would be waiting for me when I arrived, and that they'd send a car to pick me up straightaway, and it should be with me around four.

Now I knew that by the time the car arrived and I was whisked up to London there would be little time to spare, as the programme went out live at six, so I went up to my bedroom and looked out a suit – it had nothing to do with Margaret Thatcher's appearance really, but it was the nearest thing I had to her style of clothes. At least it was blue. Then the hair. Well, my own was all wrong, and so I took a wig that was amongst all my theatre bits and pieces and thought, it's not right, but it's the best I can do. Then I proceeded to do some make-up. Let's think, now. Her eyebrows – they droop at the end, mine don't, so I'll blot them out and pencil them down that way. Eye shadow – she wears pale blue. Lipstick – slightly mauve-red, and very clearly defined lips. I drew them in carefully with my lip brush, added a soft rouge high on my cheekbones – and that was that. Oh no – off with the nail varnish. I now had the suit on, the make-up was done, but I decided to carry the wig; I would give it to the make-up girl when I arrived and ask her to help me brush it into a Margaret Thatcher line. This was a very clear shape. Her hair was swept back high from the forehead into a deep kind of dent – it's the only way I can describe it – before it was brought forward in a wave, then flicked up at the sides. Later on, I always knew when she hadn't been able to make it to the hairdresser, for that dent would become deeper and deeper. Only when it is freshly done is it hidden.

I had a funny feeling that by the time the car fought its way through rush-hour traffic there'd be little time left at the studio, which is why I prepared as much as I could beforehand. All the way up to London I sat in the back of the car with my eyes closed, and I tried to recall everything I'd seen of this woman on television. The way she leaned forward in her chair when answering questions, listening with such intensity to the questioner. The look she had – I always thought of her as listening from under her eyebrows. The thing that stuck in my mind most of all was that she never, ever hesitated. Whenever she was asked a question she would answer, and the answer would come out without pauses, without any stopping. Not – 'Well, yes, er, I might say that, but ... oh er, on the other hand, this ...' I was absolutely absorbed by this.

Along with all the mannerisms I could think of, I also tried to remember as many of her remarks as possible. 'I'm a fighter, and a very determined fighter' – all the 'T's sounding like a machine-gun. The interviewer's remark, something to do with, 'Do you say that heads will roll?', and her reply, 'Heads will roll? Oh, what a *naasty* phrase.' The way she had of stretching words out. Again, when asked about forming a Shadow cabinet, and would it be quickly formed: 'Oh yes, it isn't nice to keep people waiting.' Such funny-sounding phrases they had been to me, and they'd stuck in my mind. Now I was putting them all together.

I wasn't wrong about the rush-hour traffic, it was dreadful. And by the time we reached Thames Television in Euston Road it was five to six. I'll never forget that day. I ran through the swing-doors; the make-up girl was waiting for me. I hurriedly threw the wig to her, saying, 'Can you stick some rollers in this?' and then, turning to one of the *Today* team I asked, 'Quick, quick, where's the script?' Very apologetically he replied, 'We haven't had time to write one.' Talk about being stopped in your tracks! He then went on, 'Well, we can give you some notes on idiot boards.' Now, in case you don't know, that's what they call the board they hold up out of camera with the words written on it in large letters, so that you can just read it off. That wasn't for me. 'No, never mind, I'll just talk.'

It was now six o'clock. The wig had been rolled, and brushed, and I put it on as quickly and as accurately as I could, then it was straight into the studio. Interviews were being conducted in various parts of the studio, and as I didn't go on immediately, I once again shut everything out. I had no interest in anyone else's interview. I just wanted to think myself into being her. Can you imagine the panic when no one knows what you will say or do, and the programme is going out live? While one interview was taking place, Eamonn came across and hurriedly whispered, 'What will you say?', the perspiration dampening his forehead.

I said, 'I don't know, but I know I'll talk.'

'How will you finish?'

And from wherever the thought came, I replied, 'Ask me at the end what Barbara Castle might be feeling about Mrs Thatcher's success.'

I don't think it did anything for Eamonn's blood pressure when he discovered that I'd never done an impression of Barbara Castle either. But I had watched her often enough. So, in for a penny, in for a pound.

It's a curious thing, but when you do an impersonation of someone you really *feel* yourself into the character. I don't know how other impressionists react, I only know that looking in a mirror is not for me. I have to see the picture so clearly in my mind and, like a jigsaw piece fitting correctly, the same thing happens for me – voice and mannerisms go together. And in a sense you feel taken over. It's strange, but after this particular television show I was told by Pete that I'd never looked so composed. It was conveying the style of Mrs Thatcher that did it.

I heard the interview before me come to an end, then Eamonn announcing. ... I can't now remember his actual words, but they were something to the effect that Mrs Thatcher had just won the first ballot and that, as she had been unable to get to the studio, Janet Brown had come in to give an idea of how she might be feeling. The light went on above the camera, and I was on.

I haven't a clue what I said, but I started. And as I went on, I kept bringing all the phrases that had been going through my head on the journey up to the studio. Then the most wonderful and heartening thing happened – I heard the camera boys start to laugh. I can't tell you what a lovely sound that is. Camera crews can be very tough – after all, they've seen and heard everything. Hearing their laughter in the silence of the studio helped me so much, and I kept going.

Afterwards, Eamonn asked if I'd seen him signalling to the control room before I went on. I said, 'Well, no, I was so taken up with what I had to do.'

'Well,' he said, 'I held up one finger in the hope that you'd manage a minute for us. And you spoke for three and a half. Without a script.'

Now, I know that doesn't sound a very long time, but actually when you are on your own like that, it *is* quite a time.

That was my first attempt at Mrs Thatcher, and quite honestly I didn't give it all that much thought afterwards. But the next day I found the papers had taken it up – and that was it. *Now Who Do You Do?* had already recorded a mass of Ted Heath quickies, but when Mrs Thatcher won the ballot this completely upset the applecart. Ted Heath was out, and Maggie was in. That meant *I* was in.

After that, I appeared every week in the final series as Mrs Thatcher. I certainly never thought it would lead to all the marvellously funny and odd moments that have taken place since then – or how strongly I'd be identified with her; but I soon found out. I'd go to buy a rail ticket. 'Well, Maggie, where are you off to today? Aren't you supposed to be in Germany?' I'd hail a taxi and, depending on the driver's politics, I would hear, 'Jump in, Maggie,' or, 'I'm not giving *you* a lift.' It was all good-natured fun, and I enjoyed it.

My being Mrs Thatcher appealed greatly to the press. Jean Rook of the *Daily Express* said she would like to interview me. What lovely material for another impression, I thought to myself as I took in the huge gold rings, not just on two fingers but what seemed to be on every finger on both hands, the gold chains hanging from her neck like a newly-elected Lord Mayor's, and her long blonde hair. Her voice was Yorkshire and friendly. 'Come on, kid, tell us about it,' while her pen flew over the page. She does shorthand like lightning. But it's her enthusiasm – I can see why you would pour your heart out to Jean. She is so interested in all you are telling her. She carried her own Marvel around to put into strong black coffee, which she drank endlessly while the questions fired away. I've met many interviewers since, but Jean beats them all for keenness and sheer love of her job.

'Have you met Mrs Thatcher yet?' was one of her questions.

'No,' I said, 'I haven't, but I'd love to.'

'Well, we must arrange it.'

Shortly afterwards I was on holiday in Corfu, staying in a small family hotel. One evening a bright, happy-faced woman came over to my table and introduced herself, saying did I remember we'd met in years gone by, and her name was Jill Knight. She was – still is – the Conservative MP for Edgbaston. She went on to tell me how much she enjoyed my impression of Mrs Thatcher, and asked 'Have you met her yet?' Again I said, 'No.' And she replied, 'Well, you should.'

Whatever way the wheels were put in motion, I received a letter from Jill in which she said, 'As soon as I mentioned your name to Mrs Thatcher she exclaimed, "Oh, I'd love to meet *her*. Would you bring her to tea, or drinks, or something?"'

And that is how a letter dated 15th October 1976, inviting me to Question Time and then for tea, arrived at my house.

The secretary's letter was worded discreetly:

'I presume Janet Brown would not wish for a photographer

to be present on this occasion, as Mrs Thatcher would prefer an informal meeting.'

Very diplomatically put, I thought, and immediately wrote back and said I would be delighted to come to tea.

As the date grew nearer I became like Alice, curiouser and curiouser. I wondered what it would be like meeting this woman whom I had impersonated so often. I was playing a club in Leicester that week, but I couldn't wait to get on the train and take myself to the House of Commons. I didn't feel nervous, just kind of keyed-up and expectant. Not only was I going to meet Mrs Thatcher for the first time, it would also be my first visit to the House of Commons.

I had arranged to meet Jill Knight by the side door. As I arrived the policeman hailed me with 'Who have you come to see today?', and when I said, 'Mrs Thatcher,' he replied, 'Now there's a lady that never changes. I've seen a few come and go here. Some can be very strange, but she's always the same. She always has a word with you.' It was the first comment I heard about her.

Jill was waiting to take me to lunch. What fun, sitting in the dining-room overlooking the Thames, pretending to be interested in the food when all I was really interested in was fitting names to the famous familiar faces. Question Time followed, and I was shown to my place in the Visitors' Gallery. I looked down on the scene below me. It's rather like a film set, with actors playing various parts. There was Edward Heath with his feet up. And Enoch Powell leaning back as if he was asleep. When I realized that the microphone speakers are actually at the back of the seats, I understood why so many of the MPs looked so nonchalant. They had to lean back to get their ears to the speaker, and hear all that was going on. I was absolutely fascinated. I love politics anyway, it always intrigues me to see how a question is dealt with. The skill of evading an issue, seemingly saying an awful lot while saying nothing, and the way they have of dealing with interruptions. No matter how much noise goes on in the House, the MP on his feet still clings like a rock to his last sentence. 'In my estimation . . .'

'Nonsense!'

'Hear, hear!'

'In my estimation. . . .'

Still holding on to his line he relentlessly continues. Smashing stuff!

Suddenly I was listening to a voice which sounded as if an impression of Mrs Thatcher was going on. But it was actually her. There she was. Blonde hair, powder-blue shirtwaister dress, putting questions from the Opposition bench, then sitting down while the speaker called out another name, and another MP stood up to put his question.

As soon as it was over, I was met by one of her secretaries and led down what seemed to me endless miles of corridors. Then suddenly a door was opened and I was shown into a not very large sitting-room. It's difficult to explain my feelings at that moment. Here was a woman dressed just the way I dressed when I had on my wig and suit for my impression – so for all the world it was like meeting someone else doing an impression of Margaret Thatcher – except that this time it was really her.

I don't know what I expected, but certainly not what happened. She was seated behind her desk, and as I came in she leapt up – she moves very quickly – and was round the desk in seconds.

'Come and sit down and let me take your coat. It's a bit stuffy in here.' And she proceeded to open the window.

It was all very informal. By now Jill Knight had joined us. The secretary popped her head round the door, saying, 'Oh, you're here. Right, I'll put the kettle on.' A cup of tea arrived: one biscuit on the saucer. No delicate cucumber sandwiches and chocolate cake as I'd envisaged. All very workmanlike and completely down-to-earth.

I thought she would ask me all about my impression of her, but she never mentioned it – not once. This threw me a bit, but I found later she hadn't yet seen the impression of herself, only heard from everyone else about it. At first, a lot of the conversation seemed almost 'jolly hockey-sticks'. Comments like, 'Very dull day today' – meaning Question Time – 'There were no fisticuffs'. But it was her complete interest in all I had to say that I remember so strongly. I knew I wasn't just invited for a cup of tea, and as we chatted, the questions started to come. When the red light comes on the camera, the atmosphere changes: as Mrs Thatcher said, she felt the interviewer's attitude tense up, and she felt herself tense up – did I feel this? Of course I did, I always had butterflies. As we talked, I thought what a good complexion she had, no heavy make-up. Nails plain, no varnish. On we went with questions.

Eventually I said, 'Mrs Thatcher, I'm sure I'm talking far too much.'

But the gentle voice replied, 'No please, do go on.'

I explained to her the hassle I often had with scriptwriters, depending on their political views. If they were anti-Conservative, many of the lines would be loaded, and I said how I objected to firing the bullets. And again her sympathetic reply, 'Yes, I understand, it's going against your nature.' On the other hand, how important humour was in a script, and how both sides must come in for some stick, otherwise I'd seemed too biased; and I'm not there to be political, only to entertain. Then my questions to her. I had difficulty in understanding certain parts of the House of Commons procedure. Why did she sit down after a question, instead of following on?

'Oh, if I did that, then none of my other MPs on the back benches would have an opportunity to speak.'

Two things stand out in my mind from that first meeting: one, the way she listened to what I was saying, and two, her concern that I should understand what took place in the House, and why. She reached for one of the pamphlets which explained the whys and wherefores. 'She's quite right, Jill, it doesn't make the point clear, we must have that altered.' And then she explained to me about where MPs sit in the House of Commons and their right to those positions; how Harold Wilson, coming back after retiring as Prime Minister, had to find a seat further back instead of on the front benches, because no room had been made for him by his fellow politicians.

I thought she was very honest about herself. She expressed her feelings about reading a script, said she was aware she hadn't found the knack yet, whereas Harold Wilson was an excellent reader; how she felt so much happier talking off the cuff, how she loved a good argument.

One thing made me laugh, though not out loud. In the course of the conversation Jill asked, 'Margaret, how often do you manage to get your hair done these days?' There we were, three women sitting with our cups of tea and biscuits, discussing hair-dos, in the House of Commons. I remarked, 'Mrs Thatcher, I hope you don't mind me saying so but I think the way you're doing your hair now is tons better than it was at the last conference. I think you look much younger.' To my great amusement, she leapt to her feet, glanced in the mirror, patting her hair lightly then looking at herself from under those eyebrows, and said 'Yes, well, perhaps you're right.'

I think she's very feminine, and when remarks have been made about her careful appearance I've always felt that it only tells you a little more about her disciplined mind. I can't think why you shouldn't look as good as possible, just because you work in politics. Barbara Castle has always looked immaculate with her big white collars and large bow-ties. I admire it, for I know what goes into producing the effect. I'm all for it.

After nearly an hour our conversation came to an end. I felt so much the motherliness of this woman – who on the screen had seemed to me so aloof – that I heard myself saying to her, 'Don't change too much, otherwise I'll lose a good impression.' And her smiling but clever answer as she saw me out: 'Oh, I mustn't deprive you of your livelihood.'

That evening she appeared on a television interview, and I saw her put some of the things we'd talked about into practice. Good for you, Margaret, I thought, you're having a go. I love it when people work to improve things. Just like us in the theatre, always looking for a better way to present something to an audience. Always polishing. This is what I felt she was doing, using whatever would improve her performance.

When I left the House of Commons and took a taxi to the

station the usual thing happened: 'Come on, Maggie,' shouted the driver, 'where d'you want to go then?'

And as I settled myself back in the seat, so the well-worn question came: 'Have you ever met her then? Tell you something, I reckon she's the only one who can get this country going.'

'Yes,' I shouted through the glass partition, 'I have met her.'

'What's she like then?'

I ended up on my knees, yelling into his ears over the noise of the traffic, with hardly any voice left by the time I arrived at Euston.

8

Agents And Contracts

So far I've said very little about agents. But it was obvious that I had to be looked after properly, now that so much was happening again in my career.

I first met the late Eve Taylor when she asked me to visit her office in Regent Street. Those in the theatrical profession will know immediately who I am talking about – she was one of the biggest agents in London. There was nobody like Eve, that's for sure. And I can hear every person who has ever met her echo that remark.

I was shown into her room by one of the secretaries. She was sitting behind her desk, blonde hair fluffed round her face, nails beautifully groomed with bright red nail varnish, enormous rings on her fingers, and wearing an outfit of mauve, pink and lilac – sweet pea colours – which I found later on were her favourites, and which I would see time and time again in blouses, evening clothes, day clothes – you name it, she wore it, and always combining these colours. Then she spoke. And how she spoke! She talked and talked, and finally said, 'Well, go away and think about it. Tell me how you feel about me looking after you. There are only a few I'll bother about. One thing I will say, I'm not going to promise I can do great things for you, but this I will tell you – your money will never go back.' And she was right.

I went away absolutely bewildered by all the conversation that had been fired at me over her desk, and feeling quite desperate about what I should do. All this had happened after the first series of *Who Do You Do?* Several agents had been on the phone to me. I was being asked out to lunch, asked to join their office, asked to sign their contracts – I just didn't know which way to turn. So I sat down and thought carefully of the agents who had talked with me over lunch.

'Look, Janet, you don't need me to tell you how to work. You've been in this profession long enough to know what it's all about.'

And the other approach: 'Tell me, have you done this tour, played this theatre, done this cruise ... Ah, we must do something about this.'

Well, if there's one thing you do find out in show business, it is not to believe any promises till you actually sign your contract. As my present manager said one day, 'Lou Grade's expression is, "You're never at the Palladium until they're playing your band parts".' How true that is!

But going back to Eve – I thought to myself, she hadn't made any promises, except that she would see that my money would never go back. Next day I called in to her office, and in answer to her question, 'Well, what do you think?' I replied: 'To tell you the truth, you talked so much my head was singing when I left your office, and I found it hard to think at all.'

'Right,' she said, 'this time I'll listen. My mother always said it paid to be a good listener. Now you talk.'

So I did. I told her that I'd decided I wanted her to look after me; that she might have a great deal to say to me, but when she had finished then it would be my turn to say my piece to her. And that's the way it was. Sometimes I'd get a phone call, with her voice shouting down the telephone going thirteen to the dozen. Suddenly she would stop and say, 'Are you there?' and I'd answer, 'Yes, I am. I'm just waiting till you finish.' Eventually we had a wonderful phone system:

'Eve – do you want me for anything?'

'No.'

'Right, goodbye.'

'Hang on a minute,' she said one day, 'these must be the shortest phone calls in London.'

But if there was something worth while happening or likely to happen, I can't think of any agent who would work harder or try harder for her artistes; as everyone knows, she would fight like a tiger for them. But she could be ruthless as well. I remember playing some working men's clubs in Wales, and it had been absolute disaster. The club secretary had come to me after the performance, and in this crummy dressing-room had sat down, resplendent in striped suit and spotted bow-tie, saying in a Welsh accent you could have cut with a knife, 'I don't want you to think I'm being facetious or anything, Janet, but I just want to tell you you won't be coming back to play this club again.'

And I remember saying, with great pleasure, 'Nothing could induce me to play this club again. You want a certain standard of artiste and I'm afraid I can't come down to that level.'

So I left – minus the money for the week for myself and my pianist. By the time I'd paid him out of my own pocket, I'd done less than well for myself!

Now here I was, facing Eve across the desk.

'You were fired,' she said. No words of sympathy, no 'How awful it must have been for you', just the flat statement – 'You were fired.' I felt terrible inside. But it was important to me to point out quietly that I was one of the many who hadn't stayed the course. Actually I'd lasted three days. Later on, when I was doubled up laughing about it with Little and Large, Eddie said, 'You were lucky, we only lasted two.' But the comedian Duggie Brown was the best. He said that, after he left the club on the first night and was driving along the road, he came to the roundabout and as he put it, 'One road went to Cardiff and the other went up to London, and the car just decided to go up the London road.'

That's what I love about the theatre – there are so many moments that if you didn't laugh at them you would cry. We all share this feeling – it's a great bond between artistes.

Eve it was who made me buy a fur coat.

'I don't need a fur coat, Eve.'

'Don't talk so daft! When you've a fur coat it does wonders for your morale.'

Well, I don't know about my morale but it did wonders for

my circulation when I stood on Haywards Heath station on a freezing morning, and inwardly I would bless her for her common sense. She was right too – I did feel very good, and still do when I put on my bit of mink. But there was another side to Eve, one that the business world perhaps didn't know.

'Oh no, the toast has got to be all hot and buttery – I'll do it, I'll do it.' That's how I like to think of her. We had just been to Ascot, she had taken me to Ladies' Day, my very first visit, and I'd had a wonderful time.

'We're in the Royal Enclosure. We'll be in a box.'

'Oh Eve, what fun.'

'Just look at your face – I knew you'd be pleased.'

It had been a great day. I'd seen the Royal coach and the Queen acknowledging the cheers of the crowd – that's a lovely moment, when you hear all the cheering in the distance, and then slowly you see the coach coming into view, the cheers growing louder, the toppers being waved in the air – I loved every minute of it.

Entering the box was another surprise. Men in their grey morning suits, women in all their finery, and the lunch – what an amazing sight! A table groaning under the weight of roast beef, duck, wonderful salads and cheeses, champagne, so much of everything.

But now we were back in the flat, and her first words were, 'Oh, let's get out of all this gear. Let me get my shoes off! I'm desperate for the loo. Oh, my feet are killing me.' Next, 'Do you want to get out of your togs? Right, use a dressing-gown.'

I couldn't wait. Off came the shoes, the scarlet silk suit, my hat, the lot, and on went the dressing-gown. Then, 'Well, kid, what do you fancy? Bacon and eggs?'

'No.'

'Scrambled eggs?'

'No, thanks.'

'Poached eggs on toast?'

'Oh, yes.'

'Thought that's what you'd fancy. Right, leave it to me.'

On went the pan and the eggs, and I was told to go and sit down and put my feet up. But not before she had piled cushions at my back, so that I'd be really comfy, and then I heard from the kitchen, 'Oh ow, oh ouch . . .'

I ran in and there was Eve with the toast so hot it was burning her fingers. 'That's the way it's got to be for the butter to melt and sink in.'

Never have poached eggs tasted so good as those she brought through on a tray. For my money you can keep your roast beef and Ascot box. Nobody could make poached eggs or buttery toast like Eve. This motherly side, a side which no doubt would take some believing to those who only knew her shouting down the telephone, is the side which I like to remember, and which I know her friends knew and valued.

While I was busy on the TV programmes, Pete had firmly established himself with the *Carry On* team. He played some lovely characters: I think the lunatic hotel owner in *Carry On Abroad* was one of his best, and the missionary in *Carry On Up the Khyber* another. But where were our children, you may be asking, while all this work was going on? To begin with, while I was still at home, Tyler and Emma both went to the village school, then on to boarding school. Now, please don't get the idea that this was easy for us financially. It wasn't. Many sacrifices had to be made to keep them there. Tyler had been a day boy at Cumner House Prep School in Dane Hill, a marvellously happy family school. He finally asked us if he could be a full-time boarder, as he was missing all the best bits at weekends! So we let him stay.

Emma was a day girl too, but friends were always a car journey away. Life in the country is like that. And, finally, we decided it would be better for her to go as a full-time boarder. It was much tougher on Emma than Tyler. He liked being away, and she hated it. At first journeys back after a weekend at home were awful. Her face would turn white, my stomach would be in a knot, and all the time I'd be chatting lightly about 'seeing her schoolmates again' and 'it wasn't all that long before she'd be home again'; but when the time came for the final farewell at the door, with this desolate little figure looking back at me, I would hurry round the corner and then burst into tears. Those times were tough. 'If I'd been there,' Pete said, 'I'd have had to bring her back.' So it was always me who took her. Eventually the time came when she would be dropped off at the school, run up the drive and hardly give a backward glance. Then I knew she was all right. But she never ever really liked boarding school.

Of course, there were happy times too. One of the nicest I remember is going to hear her and the other girls taking part in the *Messiah*. Seeing her flushed face afterwards, and her eyes glowing with the excitement of the evening, will always stay with me. There were other times that meant so much. My return from working once more on the *QE2*, being in the garden and suddenly hearing her voice as the back door opened; 'Mummy!' This little uniformed schoolgirl running up the garden and throwing herself into my arms, and for those few moments neither of us being able to say anything. Just hug each other.

Once I returned so exhausted from work and late nights on the ship that I passed clean out in the deckchair. In such a deep sleep I was dead to the world. I came round to find Pete holding a mirror up to my lips. 'I thought I'd better just check up that you're still with us.' Another lovely moment comes to mind – Tyler's sports day, and his dismay at missing a race he had been excitedly waiting for.

'Never mind,' said a kindly lady, 'I'll race you to the tree and back,' and she picked up her skirts and ran. I later found out she was Lady Dorothy Macmillan. I was extremely grateful to her: she made one small boy very happy that day, particularly as she let him win.

Although Pete adored the children, he was in many ways a strict father, a kind of strain of Victorianism ran through him. No matter that the schools they boarded at were not far from home, it was expected of them to write a good letter. Not 'I am out of stamps, please send money', but telling us what they did in the day. It has made both of them good letter writers. They were never encouraged just to pick up the phone because it was easier. He also had strong views on table manners. 'Elbows off the table', and 'They won't fly away, you know' if he caught them brandishing their knives and forks while telling a story, or forgetfully hanging on to them. It is only now I hear how they hated my ham soup, it was so salty, and how he would instruct them while I was in the kitchen, 'You must eat it up, pretend it's all right. Mummy's gone to a great deal of trouble, you know,' and so on.

It's not easy to recollect many of the shows I've taken part in. But I have just looked out a bunch of old contracts to see if it would help remind me.

September 1975 – Tommy Cooper Television Show.

What a funny man. At rehearsals I only had to look across at that face and it set me off.

'What are you laughing at?'

What could I say? He hadn't actually been saying anything funny, it was just that face, and the strange things he used to do. Right in the middle of a sketch – 'Now go and sit down, everyone. That's right, sit down, sit down. Now here's a glass, here's a bottle . . .' And he'd start doing some trick. It was very puzzling until I realized he was actually trying out some of his material for a cabaret he was going to do that night. A good idea, really.

Contract for *The Other Half* – oh yes, that's where I met Alan Hargreaves, the Thames Television interviewer. He was presenting the programme, and it was an interesting idea, talking about your other half. What none of us knew was that our other half was already tucked away in another studio, listening to all we were saying and ready to make a surprise appearance. Alan enjoyed the surprise it gave myself, Jean Rook, Lady Longford, and several others, but when I suddenly put him on the spot about his wife, having been put up to it by the producer, he became quite angry. Even more so when his wife suddenly appeared.

'Were those two all right?' I was asked later. 'They seemed pretty scratchy with each other.' Well, I can tell you he and Rosemary are very much all right, and again I am more than fortunate to have them as good friends. I think it was just the shock of it that caught Alan completely off guard, and oh, how the camera loves to pick up moments like that!

Here's a BBC radio contract with Roy Hudd and Chris Emmett. The BBC thought it would be a good idea to launch us as a team, and so 'News Huddlines' was born. I owe a great deal to this particular show, not least for having the good fortune to work with its producer, John Lloyd, who later went on to produce *Not The Nine O'Clock News*, following that with *Spitting Image*. He had a tremendous keenness for everything and a very sharp sense of humour.

The writers on 'News Huddlines' are too numerous to mention, but amongst them were Pete Spence, who later wrote *To The Manor Born*, Laurie Rowley, David Renwick, Chris Miller and Andy Hamilton – all excellent writers who have since helped me many times on my own television show.

It was great fun taking part in this show, for Roy, Chris and I got on like a house on fire. Chris Emmett's voices were brilliant: his Jimmy Young was the best I've ever heard. But it was the rehearsals I looked forward to most of all. Along with the producer, we'd lock ourselves into our tiny little rehearsal room, and then the dissecting of the scripts would take place. The floor was always littered with pages torn out of the script – 'That's too long, that's not good, take that out, keep that in . . .', our pencils flying over the paper, a mark here, a word underlined there. And all the time the laughs were endless while this was going on. Gladys, our lovely Gladys the tea lady, would come in with toasted buns and a cup of tea at eleven: 'Here you are, babes, drink it while it's hot.' A short stop and we were off again. You meet at nine thirty, read, cut, rehearse the script, and you're recording and in front of your audience by one o'clock. Not a lot of time. But remarkably, songs were learnt, lines changed, and a hundred per cent professional performance was pre-recorded to go out that night.

Reading through a script at rehearsals I came across a line in my Margaret Thatcher piece. 'I'm not saying this, it's too rude.'

'Oh come on, Jan, it's very funny.'

'No, no, I won't. Sorry, but no.'

The programme got under way and I reached the lines about my meeting with President Mitterand – 'Later on, we had dinner together. Afterwards he asked me if I would like to have a crêpe' – oh, I'd said the line! I'd forgotten to put my pencil through it. The laugh it raised from the audience went on and on. I stood there scarlet, and then burst out, 'I never meant to say that.' Since the programme was recorded, they were able to cut that last remark out. But Mrs Thatcher's line remained in.

Broadcasting is an art all of its own. I heard a producer say recently about some well-known comedian, 'He was excellent when he did his own act, but hopeless when he tried to read from a script.' I'd never given it that much thought – I'd just enjoyed reading from a script. But looking back I can see now the value of the experience I gained from my early days in Scotland and on all the other shows and series like 'The Navy Lark'. But if that comedian was hopeless with a script, you certainly can't say that of Roy. He has a great ebullient surging vitality – 'Life's wonderful', 'He's right on top', and 'Things are looking good' – he just sweeps you along.

I missed John Lloyd very much when he went off to join television. He was always keen that I should do my own television series, and when I finally did for Thames he wrote me a lovely letter.

Here is another contract – this time dated 1977. A cabaret for Rank Xerox. Oh yes, I remember. That's where I appeared for the first time as a surprise item at a directors' dinner.

'We'll hide you away then we want you to come on and make a speech as Mrs Thatcher.'

That was the start of hiding in rooms, hiding in lifts, hiding in kitchens. It was all great fun. I entered the dining-room, made my way to the microphone, and to my amazement they all scraped their chairs back and started to applaud. I was horrified. Good lord, I thought, they actually think it's her! I knew the kind of lines they were going to hear, and I knew they would get a surprise. But when they realized the joke, they took it very well.

Here's another contract – no, a letter this time. 'Dear Miss Taylor, We regret we are unable to use Miss Brown after all.' And a note attached from Eve. 'That's show business.'

In the Jubilee Year of 1977 I was contracted to appear with Ronnie Corbett at the Congress Theatre, Eastbourne.

'It is understood, and agreed, that the artiste should be billed full bottom in type 60 per cent of that of Mr Corbett, and no artiste shall be billed larger.' You see, even in this sort of thing you had to be protected. Billing was very important. I'd forgotten all about that.

The show was staged by Dickie Hurron, one of Delfont's top producers. True to form it had lavish sets, clever lighting, and was beautifully dressed. The Nolan Sisters were in it too, and to top it all we had the Tiller Girls. To watch them, as I did every night, walking down a great set of steps in their high heels, with their heads held high, eyes looking straight out front, wearing enormous feathered headdresses and glittering costumes, was really something. Try walking down some stairs without looking down, and you'll see what I mean. They were always given a marvellous reception.

Ronnie was a very conscientious performer. Every time I took myself into a corner to rehearse our piece, he would suddenly appear at my side. 'Want to go over it again?' And we always did.

Another contract – this time for radio, 'Just a Minute'. What a nerve-racking show that is to do! If you were to ask which was my most difficult radio show, that was it. It's all right for the usual team, but for a guest it's agony. Whether you should press the button, whether you should interrupt, what you will say when you do interrupt – oh, agony!

Here is a green stage door pass which lies on my desk – 'Royal Command Performance 1979'. But there was another Command Performance that, looking back, was more like a dream. Actually, I have just found a cutting: it was in 1975.

One day in Eve Taylor's office we suddenly had an inspiration. What a great idea it would be if I could make a surprise appearance in that year's Command Peformance. Mrs Thatcher had just returned from her first trip to the United States. Wouldn't it be fun to come on as her, wearing the black dress and the string of pearls, and make a speech. Eve, who was never one to waste time once something appealed to her, immediately got on the phone to Bernard Delfont.

'Great idea,' he said, 'marvellous. But it must be an absolute secret, and no one must know. The press mustn't get to hear about it beforehand.'

So the next day, during the rehearsal lunch-break, I furtively made my way into the Palladium, glancing hurriedly round to make sure I hadn't been seen. I met up with Bruce Forsyth in the Royal Box, and we discussed how it would work. He was compere that year, and for one link in the show he intended to do a routine bringing out the flags of all the different nations. 'Have we anyone here from Germany tonight?' for all the Germans, then he'd run off and come back with their flag. Then Israel: 'Any people from Israel?' – off again, back with the flag, and so it went on.

'Now,' said Bruce, 'I'll shout to the audience, "Is there anyone to help Britain?" and I'll get them to answer back like pantomime, shouting "Oh no there isn't," and me shouting "Oh yes there is," and at the third time you walk on from the back of the stage right down to the microphone at the front.'

It all sounded fine to me, and I was hurried out of the stage door once more without meeting or seeing anyone. I went back to Thames where I had been doing a programme: 'Could I please borrow the Margaret Thatcher wig? Can't say what it's for – tell you later.' It was such a secret.

Arriving at the theatre that night, I went to the stage door. The doorman barred my way. 'Sorry, your name's not on the list.'

'But I *am* appearing,' I told him. And I showed him my stage door admission card.

Finally it was all sorted out. I looked to see which dressing room I was in. Again a problem. And even more so when Vera

Lynn arrived. She looked at me in amazement. 'What on earth are you doing here?'

I answered rather apologetically, 'I'm in the show.'

'You can't be, we've been rehearsing all afternoon, and you certainly weren't in the finale.'

'Oh, but I will be,' I said, 'I assure you, I'm appearing. But I'm a secret.'

Vera still looked unbelieving; however, she finally accepted that I was going on.

But when? I went to the stage manager – when would I actually walk out on the stage? Having had no part in the rehearsals, I must be quite sure of what I was about. Eventually, when the show was under way, Bruce was able to give me some help. 'After this,' he whispered, and disappeared to start the routine.

I stood in the darkness, upstage, dressed in the black dress, the pearls, wig in immaculate hairstyle. My heart was thumping. Bruce's lines were building up: 'Oh yes there is, oh no there isn't, oh yes . . .'

Suddenly it was time to go on. As I walked out, there was the most awful silence. I spoke my first lines, and as the truth dawned on the audience, so the laughter came. I was thrilled. Standing in the heat of the spotlight, hearing the laughs coming back, seeing only vaguely the glitter of the jewels, the outline of furs, the whole exciting feeling of it all. Then the bow to the Royal Box, and off.

As the show neared its end and I waited for the finale, I asked where I would be in the running order. I'd been told I would be in the line-up, so I stood waiting. The names were being called out: 'Michael Crawford . . . Harry Secombe . . . Charles Aznavour. . . .' And like the old gag I kept looking at the stage manager as he clicked switches and spoke urgently through a mike – 'Is it now, now?'

'. . . Telly Savalas. . . .'

The names rang out – it couldn't be after *him* . . . Suddenly the stage was full of artistes, everyone was turning to the Royal Box: 'Three cheers for Her Majesty. . . .'

I stood at the side, bewildered. I wasn't included. 'Why

not?' I wanted to know of the stage manager.. 'I was told I would be in the line-up.'

'The line-up,' he explained, 'are those who are going to meet the Queen.' Everyone wouldn't meet her that year, but I *was* one of the ones chosen.

By this time everything had become so unreal that it was difficult to follow what was happening. The place seemed to be packed with photographers pushing and jostling. Names were being shouted out:

'Dukes and Lee ... Dad's Army ... Janet Brown. ...'

I stood with the others. The Queen stopped in front of me, and I remember her words when I spoke about the curious feeling of being someone else.

'Yes, I know what you mean. If you're not careful the character will take over.'

I suppose that's why occasionally a friend will say something on the lines of, 'Jan, don't look at me like that. You're beginning to look too sincere.'

The show was over. No parties, nothing. I put my wig back in its box, got in a taxi, returned the wig to Thames Television, and then took myself back to my flat. No one around. I was hungry. It had been a long evening. What was there to eat? Oh no! The cupboard held only a packet of soup.

I made it and sat there thinking, 'I bet the people who have been watching the show tonight think everyone is having a whale of a time.' If only they knew!

The next day the papers went on strike in London, but my friend Jean Bayliss in Birmingham informed me that I'd been given a most marvellous write-up. 'Oh, keep it for me,' I said.

'I don't think I can, darling,' she said, 'I've a feeling I've wrapped the fish scraps in it.' But she managed to rescue it, and it's in my book now with a great big yellow stripe right down my face.

It was indeed a great write-up. In the *Express*: 'Watch out for her when the show comes on your screens' – you know the sort of thing. My spirits rose again – smashing! How terrific! And then suddenly Eve on the phone. Words about 'not in the recording', 'cut out'. I was stunned. Finally, after endless calls

I managed to talk to the producer. What had happened? Well, the secret was so secret that even the television producer hadn't been told. I had come on stage and for one terrible moment he had thought it *was* Margaret Thatcher. What was she doing there? All hell let loose in the control box. It seemed I wasn't miked up for television either. There was no balance on me, and so when it came to making cuts because of the show over-running, my piece was an easy one to lose.

Later on, I sat looking at the pass admitting me to the theatre. It was all I had to show. Otherwise I could have imagined the whole thing. I had sunk without a trace. Well, there you are. Like they say – that's show business.

9

'Hold That Look'

I'm often asked, 'Who do you think is a good impersonator?' Well, there are many good ones. But I've always admired Mike Yarwood.

When the BBC suggested that he and I should meet up, I was naturally very interested. Getting together proved to be quite an experience in many ways. He was shy, hiding behind voices most of the time during rehearsals, and continually patting or pulling his hair down at the sides when reading over the lines. Come to think of it, I could have done an impersonation of him! It was only when we started sharing some laughs together, and both found a mutual admiration for what the other was doing, that he seemed to relax. In a way, it was like a tennis match with a good player. The better the lines came across to you, the more it lifted your own standard. Does that make sense? I hope so, because it's the best way I can describe how we worked together.

The scriptwriter Eric Davidson had written a sketch called 'Brief Encounter' – Jim Callaghan and Margaret Thatcher feeding the ducks together in St James's Park.

Maggie: 'You see Jim, that's the difference between us. I could never say anything unpleasant about your speeches.'

Jim: 'That's because you find them so convincing.'

Maggie: 'No, it's because I never bother to listen to them.'

Jim: 'Maggie, be serious for a moment. What's the best thing I can do regarding a general election?'

Maggie: 'Lose it.'

When I met Mrs Thatcher the second time, I told her what a laugh that last line had got. But she was so anxious to make her point that as I said the line 'Lose it', she jumped in with 'No, no, we'll win, we'll win.'

Working a double act with Mike was the beginning of many more. My Katharine Hepburn to his Richard Burton. His Eric Morecambe to my Elaine Stritch. And the one that gave us the most pleasure – his Danny La Rue to my Esther Rantzen. I was interviewing him, complete with especially made teeth, and each time Mike looked at my lips trying to make their way over those teeth he laughed so much we had to stop recording. It was said later that we complemented each other. I like to think that this was so.

Playing these other characters provided a welcome break from being Mrs Thatcher. To be in the studio, dressed in a suit and wig from early morning to late at night, was restrictive, and made me long to be myself. The moment the recording was over, I'd tear the wig off and throw it up in the air. 'Hooray! Let me scratch my head, for goodness' sake. And where's the cream to remove the make-up?' Such a relief! Whenever I go to the hairdresser, and see my hair being brushed into a wave at the side, I say, 'No, no, I don't want to look like Mrs Thatcher now. I like being myself.' It's all very well when I'm working, but being your own person is very important.

My second meeting with Mrs Thatcher took place in April of 1978, and was quite different from the first. Jean Rook rang me from the *Daily Express*.

'What do you think, kid? She's agreed to do some pictures with you at the House of Commons.'

'What, dressed like her? She doesn't mind?'

'No,' said Jean, 'she's perfectly happy about it.'

When the day came I duly arrived at Jean's office in Fleet Street. 'Wait a minute, Jean. Where do I change for all this? Do we go to the House of Commons and then I dash into a ladies' loo and proceed to put on all the bits?'

'Oh, Janet, I never thought about that one. Hang on while I find out.'

She promptly rang Mrs Thatcher's office, and was told would I please come all ready to start.

'Right,' I said, 'Here we go.' Off went my clothes and on went Mrs Thatcher's. First the bra, padded to achieve that more ample outline than mine. Oh dear! On checking through, I discovered I'd left the padding behind.

'I've got some spare tights, would they be any use?' said Jean. So I shoved these in the cups.

Next came the suit. White, trimmed with navy, exactly the same as the one I'd seen her wearing at the Conservative conference. Then the tights and shoes, black patent with a grosgrain bow. Now for the make-up. And finally I put on the wig. As I did this, Jean exclaimed in her Yorkshire accent, 'Oh God, Janet, it's uncanny. Oh, it makes me feel really odd.' I couldn't help noticing my efficient appearance was already changing the atmosphere, but I was just a bit worried that I might lean forward suddenly and find Jean's tights hanging out of the bra!

We stepped into the car. The next part was great fun. We pulled up outside the House of Commons, and the long line of people queuing to go in looked at me with enormous interest. Then they started to push towards me. We hurried into the House of Commons, and made our way down the corridors. I walked ahead while Jean and the photographer followed up behind. MPs kept passing – it was just after Question Time. I suppose they couldn't make out why Mrs T was in the corridor. The double-takes they gave amused me no end! Suddenly, instead of being shown into Mrs Thatcher's sitting room, we were directed to her office. She was standing with the door open, her back to me, giving some instructions to her secretary. As she turned, she bumped right into me. I think Jean's description of it all is the best: 'Introducing Janet Brown to Margaret Thatcher makes a big impact on you – like watching two full-length mirrors crash head-on.'

I only know I wouldn't have enjoyed it happening to me. But she didn't lose her poise. She just spoke quicker than I've ever heard her, and apart from that showed no signs of being put out.

'I like your suit, dear, it's very *à la* Mansfield.'

'It's not *à la*, Mrs Thatcher, it *is* a Mansfield.' This was the maker whose clothes she was wearing at that time, and I'd gone to great trouble to find the same one.

We then followed her into her sitting-room. She cast a critical eye over me and, spying a hairpin tucked into the wig, quickly removed it, saying, 'I never use pins.'

One thing I recollect very clearly is Jean asking, 'Margaret, do you mind if the photographer takes his picture?' She agreed quite readily. But as we settled down to talk, sitting on the sofa together, she became aware of the photographer moving around the room clicking away merrily with his camera, and she stopped right in the middle of her conversation.

'You've got your picture,' she said, 'now out you go.'

No messing about! And I can quite understand why she said it. As long as he went on taking pictures, there was no relaxing. And this she certainly did as soon as he left.

Posing for the photograph gave me some inward laughs. 'Do you mind,' I asked Mrs Thatcher, 'if I address a remark to you – speaking like you, I mean – so that the photographer can get the right expression on my face?'

'Not at all,' she said.

But as I started enunciating (in tones that, as Jean put it later, sounded like a run-down record), 'Now ... look ... here ...,' she came back with 'That's dreadful! I don't speak as slowly as that.'

'Oh, I know, Mrs Thatcher, I was just doing it slowly to hold the look.'

At one stage in the conversation I asked her how she managed to cope with all the different events of the day without wilting. And she replied, 'It's like driving. I just move into a different gear. Take myself down one when I want to relax, and move up into a higher one when it's necessary.'

There was a tremendous change from my first visit, not only because this time there was chocolate cake as well as biscuits, but also because she was so much more self-assured and in charge. It was an enjoyable meeting, with no sense of hurry about it – but when the time came for it to finish, we just knew it was time to go. A final remark to Jean about her chunky jewellery and how she, Mrs Thatcher, 'would love a belt like that, but it's much too dear', and we were outside the door once again.

As well as television appearances and the continuing radio show, 'News Huddlines', there were also the summer shows. I see from my diary that I appeared at Bridlington in the summer of 1978, this time with Les Dawson. I'd met up with Les many times, but this was the first time we'd shared a season together. Rehearsals were a panic, the band in the pit helpless with laughter. And as for me – trying to get the words out in a sketch was almost an impossibility. He and Pete both had what I call a 'chunky' look, and it wasn't unusual to find Pete being approached and asked to 'give us your autograph, Les,' and vice versa. Stu Francis was the other comedian in the cast. He had a very likeable, cheeky personality. Obviously the BBC thought so too, because he went on to head the team of the well-known children's television programme, *Crackerjack*.

The house that I stayed in that year was at Flamborough Head. The first night I returned to it after the show I got the fright of my life. When I put my key in the door, the whole house lit up. . . . I'd forgotten about the famous Flamborough lighthouse!

One of the nice things about a summer show is the new friends you make. I soon found out what a fine lot of people my neighbours were. When they asked me if I would open their RNLI fête for them I was only too happy to oblige. We had a great day together. The young boys of the village did their traditional sailors' dance, I judged the most beautiful baby competition – making sure, of course, someone helped me with this tricky task – and finally ended up buying all the home-made marmalade I could find. Oh yes, it was a marvellous day. The Flamborough lifeboat crew and their wives became my friends, and I still hear from them at Christmas.

I've just come across another note in my diary – I suppose I scribbled it in because it made me laugh so much at the time. All the cast were invited to one of the hotels after the show, and they had publicized it in the local press in a big way. There was a huge ad which said: 'Big Night Out – Come and Meet the Stars. Les Dawson, Janet Brown, etc.', and in the corner: 'Pie and Mushy Peas Will be Served'. I loved that!

I think it was at that party that I first met Michael Barrymore. He was playing the other theatre, and had been experiencing a bit of a rough time – not with his show, but just with things in general. Later on, I met up with him again when he was the warm-up studio comedian for the Mike Yarwood show. The audience loved him. He was good-looking, very funny, and no one could have been more delighted than I was when everything started happening for him. He deserved it.

Tyler didn't manage a trip to Flamborough that summer. He had gone to Edinburgh to work with Jeremy Taylor and his children's theatre. But Pete and Emma were able to stay with me for a little while. We had some lovely days together, walking along the cliffs with the waves dashing below while the seagulls wheeled overhead. Yorkshire is such a beautiful part of the country: it has to be one of my favourite places. I never tired of the scenic drive to York when I went over to pick up friends from the station, and I always insisted that they see Sledmere House, the home of the Tatton Sykeses. It was full of charm, with glorious views. The name 'Tatton Sykes' must have amused Pete. He, Emma and I were wandering around the grounds one day, and came to the small café there where nice friendly country ladies serve you tea. While Emma wasn't looking he stuck a little note on an Eccles cake, and as she went to eat it she saw the note. It read: 'Who from this Eccles cake bites, Will be the next Lady Tatton Sykes'.

'Daddy!' Her face was red with embarrassment. And then we all dissolved into laughter.

It's silly I know, but it is one of those happy family

moments that occasionally we bring up and laugh at all over again.

Many friends came to stay with me at Flamborough Head, including my Mrs Scott, who you may remember took care of our home for us. Took care is an understatement. If there was a pillowcase to be mended, a hole in Tyler's jeans, a much-needed kitchen utensil to be bought – she always saw the need and did something about it. Throughout the years she had cycled round to us on her bike. 'I feel safer on it than walking,' she would say. Once in the house, she never wasted a minute. My favourite story about her concerns the day of Lord Mountbatten's funeral. Tyler was watching it all on television, and he called out, 'Mrs Scott, stop working, you must see this, it's history.' So she came in and sat down on the sofa, and as the cameras moved from the crowds and the marching soldiers it slowly panned to the face of Big Ben.

'Oh my word,' cried Mrs Scott, jumping up, 'just look at the time and I haven't even done the brass yet!'

I love her dearly, and certainly I would never have been able to do the work I have done had it not been for her constant help. A wonderful woman, who despite all she has had to cope with, has somehow still managed to laugh at life's adversities.

So many friends came to see me at Flamborough Head that I began to feel like a holiday landlady. 'I'll just see if I have any vacancies,' was the usual line when they rang. It was great to see them, for they all brought their own warmth and humour. Sheila Holt was one of them, a beautiful dancer whom I had worked with on the QE2, and who, after a dreadful car accident, had the spirit to fight her way back. She was still coping with the aftermath of operations, and arrived limping along the platform at Bridlington with an enormous great bandage covered in polythene on her foot.

'What on earth's that for?'

'To keep the rain off it,' she said cheerfully. It should have been a serious moment, but we both stood there helpless with laughter. She looked for all the world like the little fellow on the end in the comedy band routine – someone's always hitting his damaged foot with a stick and asking, 'Is that the one that hurts?'

Betty King was another friend who came to stay. She runs our local winery.

'I haven't brought any wine with me, for I'm not drinking,' she stated firmly. I didn't mind, I don't drink anyway. But in the early evening, when I suddenly remembered the sherry in the cupboard, I said casually, 'Would you like a glass, Betty?' She leapt up with desperation in her voice – 'Yes please! I thought you were never going to ask me.'

I remember calling at her cottage in Sussex one summer's day, and while we were chatting my eyes suddenly alighted on a mince pie nailed to an old oak beam.

'Oh yes,' she said airily, when I mentioned it, 'it's been there since Christmas.' That's Betty!

Between laughs with my friends at the house, and laughs with Les at the theatre, it was a very happy summer season.

10

Finding The Way Back

In January of 1979, Pete died. Funny, but I have been rather dreading writing this part – maybe because a certain part of me and my life and family wants to be kept to itself. It's also the first time I will actually have put down in print the awful moment when I first heard what had happened.

Tyler and I had been up in town in Harrods, looking at coats in the Men's Department. I think now of me and my practical Scottish outlook. 'Marvellous coats, aren't they?' he said. 'I would love one like that.'

'But you've got a coat,' I replied.

He looked at me. 'Oh yes – but I'd love to open the wardrobe door and see several!' I'd never thought that way.

We came back to the flat and the phone rang; a call from the stage door of the theatre in Coventry where Pete was playing in pantomime. I knew something was terribly wrong before I was even told what had happened. I felt this terrible cold feeling in my stomach – a sort of struggling for breath, trying to speak normally and with control. Peter had had a heart attack, the voice was saying, and had not appeared in the theatre for the matinee. He had been found in his hotel room.

The rest is too painful, even now, to go into detail about. There are times when you hear stories about theatre people – about their behaviour – how shallow or self-centred they can be. I haven't found that, and the night Pete died demonstrated very forcibly to me how kind they can be. I was surrounded by help: Danny La Rue was appearing at the Palladium in pantomime where he had heard the news – how he knew so quickly I don't know – and within moments he had called, saying there was a rail strike and I might have a problem getting to Coventry, so he'd put his car and chauffeur at my disposal. My friend Jean Bayliss in Birmingham was on a train and with us in no time at all. Dear Jean! She came complete with a loaf and an enormous piece of roast beef – she just knew there would probably be little in the flat, which was only a work base really, and as well as putting things right with food she was there to help and look after us all.

Pete left such a wonderful sense of humour with us, there's no doubt it rubbed off strongly on Tyler and Emma and on me and we clung to that – no sad house – no dreary faces – but it's not that easy. In the end I had to take myself off for a week. I simply had to get away from the endless phone calls, the repeated explanations to kind friends who rang, the steeling of emotions to sound calm and in control. Tyler and Emma were trying hard to cope with their feelings too – and the unreality of everything. Letters came from everywhere: from viewers, friends, even from Australia and America where children, long since grown up, remembered with great affection this man they had known so well from his many children's television appearances. *Pete's Troubles* had been a particular favourite, and they still had a clear picture of him wearing his bowler hat and trying to boil a kettle over a candle!

I went to Majorca, and on the second day I was sitting in a restaurant when Harry Secombe and his wife Myra walked in. I'm everlastingly grateful to them. Harry made me laugh, lots, and they enfolded me in their generosity and love and I came back feeling I could cope with things again.

I won't write on about Tyler and Emma. Anyone with a family reading this will understand only too well the pain of this time in our lives. Now we can roar with laughter and talk about things we all shared, but at that time it was very hard.

I found long after Pete died that we were still thought of with concern. Jimmy Jewel, one of Tyler's godfathers, rang every week – were we all right, he wanted to know – was there anything we needed? I loved Jimmy for that and the calls continued until he knew we were really finding our way back to a more normal state of life.

I have very strong feelings about death. I felt that all the laughs and the humour, the gentleness and fun that was Pete couldn't die: these qualities are always there and I feel we are still, the three of us, within that warmth.

I once said to a friend of mine how relentless life is – nothing stops. Even in the saddest moments you have to put the kettle on and make a cup of tea – walk the dog, buy food – you're just pushed into keeping going. I knew that even the best of friends can only give you their sympathy for so long and then they too must get on with their lives and I knew I must get on with mine.

Appearing again on television in *Blankety Blank*, my first show after Pete's death, was difficult. Walking across the studio floor in front of a studio audience and making my way to my place on the panel took great effort. Trying to fit in with the mood of the show, to laugh and joke was even more difficult. I felt the strain terribly – but this thing of being forced to get on with things came to the top and I managed. It was only later, when I talked with Alan Boyd (then the programme's producer) that I found once again everyone involved had wanted to help; they'd all been aware of how hard it would be for me, so soon. For Emma and Tyler, too, it was a period in which they each had to try and find their own way back. I never realized more the meaning of the word 'family' than I did then. If I went down they picked me up and I hope I was able to do the same for them.

I suppose I threw myself into whatever work was offered me, though I hadn't really realized just to what extent until I looked back at my diaries. There was television, radio and cabaret. Then in May, Mrs Thatcher won the election, and became Prime Minister.

The evening of the election, I was appearing in cabaret at the Hilton Hotel in London. What an extraordinary night it turned out to be! Enormous television screens had been placed in the cabaret room so that the diners could watch the results as they came in from all over the country. Earlier I had done my usual cabaret spot, but as midnight approached, I changed out of my evening dress into my Mrs Thatcher suit and wig. A straightforward announcement was made to the audience that in the midst of everything Mrs Thatcher had taken time away from her North Finchley constituency to spare us a few moments. I walked into the spotlight to the strains of 'Land of Hope and Glory'. There was tremendous applause and cheering from one side of the room where the Conservative supporters were sitting, and from the other side an equally loud booing, which informed me in no uncertain terms where the Labour supporters were.

I was completely accepted by the audience, and such was the feeling of excitement that when I suddenly decided to do a Mrs Thatcher walkabout and make my way round the tables, to my amazement people leapt to their feet, running forward to shake hands with me. All this excitement, of course, was enhanced by the fact that several television companies from home and abroad were there, running around and following me with their cameras. I suppose it gave the whole thing an atmosphere of reality. It just surprised me that such was the power of illusion, it could actually create this fervour amongst the audience, who ended up standing and singing 'Land of Hope and Glory' as I went off. It was the strangest feeling, and one of the most amazing nights I've ever experienced. For a moment I felt as if *I* had been elected Prime Minister.

I was much too excited that night to sleep, and besides I had a television interview with *Nationwide* the next morning at seven o'clock, so I sat up till dawn in my hotel room. The scriptwriter Neil Shand had provided me with both a winning and a losing speech. Happily it was the winning one I was able to use.

At the studio that election morning, all was controlled chaos. As Sue Lawley introduced me, a thought suddenly said: 'Take your script with you.' It had been put on autocue, and I really didn't need to take it – but I did, just the same and just as well! For as the camera moved into position I saw to my horror that there was no autocue there. I would have been completely without my winning words.

Later I sent Mrs Thatcher a note of congratulations, and received the following letter back:

10 DOWNING STREET

17th May 1979

Dear Janet Brown,

Thank you very much indeed for your kind letter.

I half expected to arrive in Downing Street and to find that you were here before me! Although you were not, I hope to meet you again before long.

With best wishes,

Warm regards

Yours sincerely

Margaret Thatcher

Janet Brown

As a matter of fact, we have corresponded since 1975; some of the letters are hand-written, and in others typed by her secretary she has added her own little notes. I truly don't know where she finds the time.

I have had many funny moments as Mrs Thatcher. Only recently I was asked to make a speech at a business conference – a working breakfast actually. Now, half past nine in the morning isn't the easiest of times to be addressing an audience, particularly when some of them are recovering from a late night! I walked on to the platform and placed my notes on the lectern.

'We don't like you,' an Irish voice from the front row proclaimed.

From the others came polite applause. I launched into my script, and as they realized that the lines were not political, and that it was all just a joke, so they laughed. But such is the authority of the woman that at one point, when one of the men produced a camera, I said in my coldest Mrs T tones: 'If you intend to take a picture, would you kindly wait till I have finished my speech?'

The effect was immediate. You've never seen a camera disappear so quickly. At the end of the speech as I was leaving the platform to make my way through the audience, the same Irish voice from the front row shouted: 'You're all right, Maggie, come and give us a kiss.'

I stopped to chat on the way out and noticed that one of the men had a cigarette in his mouth. I addressed him sharply: 'Are you in the habit of smoking in the presence of the Prime Minister?' In seconds it was out of his mouth and under his foot. Of course, it's all just fun, but it does give you an idea of how strongly people react, or believe in the character you are impersonating. Once I boarded an aircraft, and shortly after take-off the stewardess came to me. 'Will you,' she said, 'just for a joke, come up to the flight deck and do a Mrs Thatcher to the pilot?' My immediate reaction was to say, 'Oh please, no, I'd just like to sit quietly and take time off for a while,' then I heard what she had done. She had gone to the pilot and said, 'Guess who's on board? Mrs Thatcher!'

'Nonsense. She's in hospital having her legs operated on.'
(This was for varicose veins.)

'I know. But didn't you see this morning's picture? She's out, and she's sitting at the back of the aircraft.'

The pilot, in more ways than one, went into a flat spin. 'Tidy up the flight deck. No, wait a minute, give me a duster – now bring her up. No, hang on, let me fasten my collar. Get rid of that magazine.' And so on. Finally he said, 'Right, right, you can bring her through now.'

When I finally came in and breathed down the back of his neck, 'Good morning', the laugh of relief was really heartfelt.

Travelling around as I do, and meeting people who in turn have met her, I hear some interesting stories. Nice ones, too. For example, I heard from a consultant that on a day when she was presenting awards to nurses, she stopped after every one of more than forty presentations so that the photographer could take his picture of her and the nurse. Afterwards the consultant remarked to her how impressed he was with her speech, particularly as she hadn't been looking at her notes. She explained that she had flash blindness from the camera's continual flash, and so she had been unable to see a thing. On another occasion, when she had finished making a political broadcast, she took time when it was over to see that all the daffodils that had been provided as a background would go to hospitals and not just be left to die in the studio heat.

In the summer of 1979 I made an LP called *The Iron Lady*. It was written by John Wells of *Private Eye* fame (amongst other things, he does such a funny Denis Thatcher), and produced by John Lloyd, my producer from 'News Huddlines'. While recording, I had a bit of difficulty with some of the words. It was my Scottish accent again.

'Can you help us, Janet?' John Lloyd said carefully. 'You see, when you sing Iron Lady, it's coming over with a very strong "r" sound. The "Eyerron lady".'

John Wells then suggested that I try singing I-on Lady, which I did. 'They call me the I-on Lady'. It worked. I still think you should hear the 'r' sound. I can never understand why George Formby should be pronounced George Fomby –

but if that's what is wanted, who am I to argue. Never mind, in Scotland I can say I-ron, and For-umby, and it will be quite all right.

The publicity man handling the promotion of the record rang me to say he had arranged for me to go to Brighton, where the Labour Party Conference was in session. Everyone, he told me, was quite happy about it. The Labour politicians attending would be delighted to have some pictures taken with me at the hotel where they were all staying. What? Me, dressed as Maggie, at the Labour Conference hotel? 'Are you sure?'

'Absolutely. I'll pick you up and we'll drive down there early tomorrow.'

We arrived at the hotel, me with the suit, blouse and of course the wig box – that was the most important item – and up we went to the room where I was to change. When I was ready and satisfied that my blonde hair looked immaculate, I said, 'Right. Now who am I to be photographed with?'

'Oh well,' he responded rather breezily, 'we'll just play it off the cuff.'

'How do you mean? Haven't there been any proper arrangements made?' By this time I was less than happy about the whole affair and really quite angry, because I felt I had been conned into doing it. Well, I was there. So what next?

'Let's just go down into the foyer,' he said. 'All the journalists are there.'

Oh, this was so embarrassing. I was being pushed into goodness knows what. We walked into the foyer. There were the press, and there was a great deal of good-natured laughter as I approached and said 'Good morning' in Maggie's voice. In no time at all they were clustered, chatting, around me. Suddenly there was a kind of buzz about the MPs who were coming through the swing-doors, and one of the press photographers said, 'Let's get a picture of you greeting some of them as they enter.' I was really feeling very bad by now, and I replied, 'No, no, it's much too embarrassing.' But as they backed away, I was left, stranded in the centre of the foyer, on my own, rather like the 'volunteer' in the army. (You know – 'Who's going to volunteer, I want you, you and you.') Just then the revolving door spun round, and in walked Roy Hattersley. With nowhere else to go, I swallowed hard. 'Good morning, Mr Hattersley.' I was given a sharp push on the shoulder and the reply, 'If I want any publicity, I'll do it my way.'

I can't tell you how awful I felt. Right, that's it, I thought, I'm going home. I'm not going to humiliate myself with situations like this. But by this time my PR man was out of the door and shouting to the people outside: 'Mrs Thatcher's here!' Perhaps the craziness of it all just got to me, for I found myself waving from the steps. Women across the other side of the road ran over to me. 'Good old Maggie,' they shouted. I stood with my arms high above my head, as she does, while the banner over the hotel entrance stated that the Labour Party Conference was being held there. It was really quite mad, but I'm happy to say that many of the Labour Party entered into the spirit of it all. And so I posed for pictures with John Silkin, who was charming, and with Clive Jenkins, who joined in the fun with a great twinkle in his eye, and Manny Shinwell, who shouted 'Come and sit on my knee, Maggie, while I give you a kiss.' He told me that he thought Maggie was a great girl.

Later, I made a point of finding Roy Hattersley to tell him that it was not my idea to greet him as he entered. He said, 'I'll accept your apology only if you will accept mine.' I'm glad that moment was cleared up.

The next item on the agenda was a meeting with Barbara Castle in a hall near the hotel. As I walked in I saw this red-haired woman seated at a table, wearing a rather strange hat on her head and holding forth in a kind of Margaret Thatcher voice. Neil Kinnock and Joan Lester were there too. Everyone was very friendly. I suppose I must have looked puzzled, because after I had been introduced to Barbara Castle, she explained that she was practising her impression of Mrs T for the review the MPs were giving that evening.

She invited me to lunch at the hotel, along with her husband

Ted. I remember she was quite concerned about everything at the table being just right. During the meal she talked about the review, and then said, 'I wonder if you could give me some tips for my impression of Margaret. I used to do it quite well, but I've got a bit rusty. If you could just refresh my memory.' That struck me as being a little odd; after all, she did see Mrs Thatcher every day in the House, but I said I'd be very happy to help, and we chatted on.

I was fascinated by her expression 'coun-ter-pro-ductive', delivered in her decisive Yorkshire accent. It was obviously one of her favourites, because she used it several times – 'I don't see the point in that, it's coun-ter-pro-ductive.' I thought, I must use that the next time I do a Barbara Castle impression. Have you noticed, by the way, the difference between the two women when they give a television interview? Mrs Thatcher always addresses the interviewer very formally – 'May I just say, Sir Robin' or 'Mr Burnett'. Barbara Castle has a different approach, as if she wanted to be in the interviewer's good books. 'Now look here, Robin, you know as well as I . . .' – that sort of thing.

Suddenly, between the main course and the sweet, she asked, 'Have you met Jim and Wedgy?' I said, 'No, I haven't, but I'd love to.' The next minute I was led round to Jim Callaghan's table, and after the first slight jump he was very affable. After all, I was still dressed as Maggie! Tony Benn was charming and very complementary about my impression but preferred not to pose for pictures, when asked to by the photographers. Can you imagine the scene? The dining-room full of Labour MPs, and me sitting with Barbara Castle, complete with the oufit, blonde wig and make-up on – it struck me as being very funny.

The final touch came when Barbara asked if I would come up to her bedroom 'so that I can get help with the impression in greater detail'. The bedroom surprised me somewhat. 'I don't know why,' she said, 'but every time I come to this hotel they give me the bridal suite.' So we sat in the presence of a large four-poster bed draped heavily with white lace, and I proceeded to try and help her. 'I must explain,' I pointed out,

'I never know what my face does when I impersonate someone, I never look in a mirror. It might be better if I just read the script as Mrs Thatcher, and you can see what mannerisms take place.'

'That's a good idea,' she said, and promptly sat down right in front of me, pad and pencil at the ready. I launched into her script and she scribbled away, making comments – 'Oh yes. Left eyebrow down, hands together . . .'

There was a knock at the door. 'Time for the executive meeting, Barbara.'

'I'll be with you in a minute,' she said, 'but first I must get my impression right for tonight.' The priorities are interesting, aren't they?

Before I left this friendly woman, I offered to leave her one of my wigs to use that night in the review if she would arrange to send it back to me.

There was a lovely moment when I said, 'You know, I don't really look like this, my hair-style is completely different.' She'd gone into the loo and when she came back I'd taken my wig off. 'Why,' she exclaimed, 'you look sweet. You're not the least bit like her!'

Another November had come round, and with it an invitation to appear in the Royal Command Performance. Once again I was to be a secret, but not this time as Maggie. This time I was to be Carol Channing. Carol was appearing at Drury Lane Theatre in *Hello Dolly*. I'd been impersonating her in my cabaret act, and had loved her ever since I'd seen her some years earlier in her one-woman show in London. The word 'star' is used so easily these days, but Carol Channing epitomises for me what that word really means. When she walked on to the huge stage at Drury Lane, radiant in white evening gown and swathed in furs, with a kind of eager expectancy about her, the effect on the audience was immediate. She captivated them.

Everyone, including Carol, thought the idea of doing an impression of her was a good one. A meeting was arranged at

Miss Channing's flat. I say Miss Channing, for when I arrived
at her flat and was waiting for her to come into the room, her
husband Charles Lowe kept referring to 'Miss Channing' this,
and 'Miss Channing' that. It sounded rather strange to me –
after all he was speaking about his wife! Then the door
opened, and in walked Miss Channing. I hadn't been prepared
for such a tall lady – she's five foot nine, but as I found later on
she wears low heels, and big 'Quaker' collars to her dresses,
and so appears smaller. Anyway, here she was, and I think
without exaggerating I can use the phrase, 'looking larger than
life.'

'Why, hell-ooo.' The voice was exactly the same as I'd heard
it on stage. But it was her eyes. They were *enormous*. The
biggest eyes I've ever seen. And she had on her full make-up
because she was going to the theatre for the matinee of *Dolly*.
She was wearing a scarlet dress with a big white collar, black
bow and little red boots; above the enormous eyes, a blonde
wig with an enormous fringe. She was warm and friendly, and
I said straight away, 'May I call you Carol? And I'm Janet.'
There, we'd got rid of the 'Miss Channing', and life was much
easier.

I explained how I hoped to copy her, and she immediately
suggested I might like her wig from *Dolly*, and the dress. No,
that wasn't what I had in mind. I'd seen her on the Parkinson
show looking marvellous in a cream-coloured taffeta and lace
dress and a blonde wig like the one she was wearing. That's
how I saw myself doing it. She was helpfulness itself, and
immediately went and got her wig box.

'I've got a spare one – here we are, now try it on.'

I did, and it went right down over my eyes. I have a small
head and features, that's one of the problems when wigs are
being made for the characters I play. They look fine on the wig
block, but they always have to be flattened down so as not to
overwhelm me. Back to Carol and her wig. She searched
around for some tissue paper, and stuffed that into the crown,
and things began to look much better. She said she would help
me with the make-up. Then she fetched the dress. It was so
pretty, and we arranged to have it copied.

Now how was this idea to be presented? Scriptwriter Dick Vosburgh, Carol and I sat around with cups of coffee chatting about it. And finally Dick came up with this suggestion: I should walk on from one side of the stage looking as like Carol as possible – her double really – and my conversation to the audience would be along typical Carol Channing lines – 'Whyeee, helloooo everybody. How wonder-ful to be in lovely, lovely London.' And then she would come on from the other side, see herself and rather like her. Carol's dialogue was to be along these lines:

'Whyee! Isn't she swe-et! I don't know who she is, but I like her. I like her hair, I like her clothes . . .' More of this sort of thing, and after meeting centre stage, and both saying 'Why, hellooo Carol', Carol would add: 'Do you know, I met the Prime Minister the other day, and do you know what she said to me?' I had to answer, 'Yes I do', and follow it with the tones of Mrs Thatcher.

Suddenly it dawned on me at this point that I would finish the piece with Carol, exit singing 'Hello Dolly' and no one would know who it was. Carol was quick to agree this wasn't right, and on the night, after the Mrs Thatcher line, she burst forth with: 'Whyee! It's Janet Brown!', her face a mixture of surprise and delight.

She was a hard worker. I think most American artistes are. They have great stamina. As I was a secret, the only way we could rehearse together was after the show at night, which meant going back on stage after 11 o'clock – and on the day of our first rehearsal she'd already done a matinée of *Dolly*, and the evening performance (and if you've seen the musical you'll know that Dolly, the main character, is on stage a great deal). No one was around, all the cast had gone; and in the quiet of the theatre and on that great big stage, we rehearsed our piece. We got on really well together. She and her husband Charles called me 'Little Janet' – 'Whyee, hello, Little Janet' Carol would say in that husky cracky dark-brown voice, and I really did feel little, especially when she stood next to me.

On the day of the show I managed to slip into the theatre without any of the other artistes seeing me, and I made straight for Carol's dressing-room. I was completely hidden away. The make-up was all-important, and so we started. She was generosity itself, and had cleared her own dressing-table for me to sit at, while she made do with a long mirror and a chair to put her bits and pieces on.

'No, I insist, Little Janet. Now here's your make-up,' – pulling open a drawer – 'and there are your lashes,' – another drawer opened – 'and here's your stocking to put over your hair.' In case you didn't know, it's quite a common thing to wear a kind of stocking-top cap to keep all your hair ends in before putting on a wig.

I hadn't a clue how to do her make-up, so rather like painting by numbers we began, and I watched my face disappearing and that of Carol slowly appearing. First there was a special all-over base. And then the placing of the rouge – this was quite extraordinary. A bright dot was placed high on each side of my nose. Then the shading of the eyelids, and the applying of the huge false eyelashes, top and bottom.

Jon Scoffield, who was directing the television side of things, came to me at rehearsals. 'Something's not quite right,' he said. 'Your bottom lashes are not the same as Carol's.' And indeed they weren't. She had to find the exact copy so that the effect was correct. It's details of this kind that make all the difference, and I was grateful to him for noticing.

Next I drew in a mouth, carefully following the lines of Carol's. But the best part was giving me a turned-up nose. She showed me how to do this, with clever shading. Then finally her hairdresser placed the wig on my head. Suddenly I had gone, and Carol was there. When all was finally finished – dress on, make-up done, wig filled with tissue – and I was looking just right, she said in a surprised voice: 'Why, you look cute! Just like my father in drag!'

We stood looking in the mirror together – it really was quite remarkable. The turned-up nose was such a contrast to my own and I burst out laughing at the image looking back at me. This was going to be fun! Carol obviously thought so too. Whoever came into the dressing-room had to sit down immediately while we did our act for them. I realized it was Carol's way of rehearsing, and that was fine by me.

Charles said at one point, 'Janet, you're like George Burns, you rehearse right down to the last puff of the cigar.'

He was concerned about me and my food. Earlier on Carol had offered me some of hers.

'Help yourself, Little Janet,' and then handed me a huge raw carrot. I sat there politely munching it, but it was more than I could cope with. I didn't know then that she was into all kinds of unusual eating habits. She even takes her own bottle of water to restaurants.

Was I hungry, Charles enquired anxiously. 'I'll fetch you a steak, or how about some chili?' I didn't feel I could manage either, because I felt pretty keyed-up. He left the dressing room and shortly afterwards appeared with a beautiful silver tray filled with tiny smoked salmon sandwiches.

'Oh, just perfect, Charles,' I said. 'Where did you get these from?'

'I found them in the Royal Box,' he answered. 'I reckon you need them more than the Queen, after all, you're working!'

Finally the show started. There's always tremendous excitement backstage at a Royal Command Performance; there are television monitors covering the departure of the Queen and Prince Philip from Buckingham Palace, the arrival outside the theatre, and finally the entrance into the Royal Box. Throughout the evening you hear the names of the performers being called through the tannoy in the dressing room, as each artiste is required on stage.

'Miss Channing and Miss Brown on stage please.' It was our turn.

We stood at the side – both of us had such a good feeling about it. And as the music started I walked on, my arms outstretched, eyes looking right out and up to the gods. 'Whyeee, hellooo everybody . . .'

As the audience realized it was a send-up they broke into applause and laughter. I said that Carol was tall, but I hadn't reckoned on her wearing high heels. She entered from the other side saying her lines, then met up with me centre stage.

She towered above me! But as we sang and exited together to tremendous applause we both felt elated. Everything had gone marvellously.

I remember a journalist asking me once for one of my happiest moments. Well, that has to be one. Not because I was in the Royal Command Performance, but because Tyler and Emma were there. When I found on the kitchen table next morning a little note from Tyler, saying: 'You were terrific last night, Mummy', that meant more than any write-up ever could. Compliments are not thrown about in our family, so I knew it must have been all right.

Christmas was approaching with its Christmas shows, and I was asked once again to team up with Mike Yarwood. There were some lovely funny sketches. 'Celebrity Squares' was one. Between us we supplied the panel. Mike did, amongst other impressions, his Bob Monkhouse, which I think is hilarious. And I included a new one of Marti Kane. Another item we did together was a double of Anna Ford and Reggie Bosanquet reading the news. I spent over two hours in the make-up chair being made into Anna Ford. At the end of it all I was quite depressed. 'I don't really look all that different,' I said to Mike as I studied myself in the mirror.

'Ignore the mirror,' said Mike comfortingly, 'and wait till you see yourself in the monitor.' When I did I was greatly relieved. The make-up girls had done an excellent job, and I did look like her after all. Anna Ford had seemed to me to have a kind of identikit face – wide across the forehead, and then coming down to a very pointed chin. And her voice was low and slightly husky. She had an interesting way of saying the word 'problem'. It came across as I was watching her on the news one night, and so I started with that, talking away to myself as I put the kettle on. 'This is a very difficult problem' – no, no, not quite right. Listening in to myself when I am trying out a new character is one of the things I do a great deal of. I try and remember as much of the person and their mannerisms as possible, along with any strong characteristics in their voice, and I recall them mentally, and I listen inwardly. Then I try them out loud. Anna always sat very straight, looked right into camera and barely moved her head. She wasn't at all easy to do, and I'm sure I must have driven the family mad when I was practising this new impression by continually repeating her sentences, just one beat after she had said them.

On the night of the television it all worked well, and I had one more voice to add to my list.

In between the television shows, there were still cabarets and conferences. One that will forever stick in my mind was the ASLEF centenary. I had been booked as the guest speaker, but the delegates had no inkling about who the guest would be. I can see it all now: on stage was the Grimethorpe Colliery Band, and behind them the banners. As I walked into the spotlight in my Mrs Thatcher outfit and made my way to the lectern, the place broke into an uproar.

'Get off! Get off!' they chanted. And 'What about the twenty-five per cent?'

It was impossible to speak! And almost impossible to keep a straight face. 'This is great!' I thought, as I continued to wave happily to the audience, which only incensed them more. And then, as the noise died down a little, I started my speech. When they realized what was happening, their angry mood changed to one of laughter. Bill Owen (of *Last of the Summer Wine* fame) was the organizer of the event, and he had given me several special lines to say. I'd no idea what they meant, but I've no doubt Mrs T would never have said them. Not if the laughs they got were anything to go by!

When I came back to take my call, Ray Buckton – who was sitting in the front row – stepped forward and kissed my hand. What a picture that would have made for the press! Ray Buckton pays homage to Mrs T.

Afterwards some of the audience came round backstage. 'I'm sorry, but I can't shake hands with you,' one stony-faced woman remarked. 'You're too much like the real thing.'

Christmas at home was our first Christmas without Pete, but we went ahead with our usual morning drinks party and friends came in as always. I know it must have been painful for them, but I have good friends, and along with Tyler and Emma who, like me, went all out to make it a happy day, we managed very well. There have been many times when I have been overwhelmingly grateful to them both, and this was one of them.

February came along, and so did Tyler's twenty-first birthday. For a long long time he had talked about a Mini-Moke, how marvellous he thought they were, how wonderful it would be to own one, and so on. On his birthday morning there were just the two of us in the cottage. When Mrs Scott arrived to perform her usual miracle with the well-worn line: 'I think we're beginning to get straight now,' Tyler was a bit subdued. After wishing him happy birthday, I said, 'Hold on while I go through to fetch your present from the other room.' Actually what I was doing was phoning my next-door neighbour.

'Quick, Pat,' I said. 'Can you get it outside the house now?'

I walked back into the kitchen. 'Oh, Tyler, just bring in the milk would you, and we'll have a cup of coffee.'

He opened the door to bring in the milk, and there was the Mini-Moke, gleaming and shining, green and cheeky-looking, sitting in the lane. I shall never forget his face. He was white.

'Good Lord, there's a Mini-Moke!'

'It's yours, Tyler.'

'Oh, Mummy!' He picked me up and whirled me round. 'Mrs Scott, quickly, look, just look!'

Talk about tears in the eyes! I don't know who was worse.

'Get in,' he ordered.

'What, now?'

'Yes, now!'

'Right!'

And off we went up the lane, hair flying, nothing on our feet, he in his pyjamas and me in my dressing-gown. What we looked like, goodness knows. But who cared? It was another of my happiest times.

11

It Really __Is__ A Surprise

It was during the early part of 1980 that Thames Television approached me about doing my own television special. It was very exciting news. We had meetings with Philip Jones, Head of Light Entertainment, and he asked if there were any particular writers I would like to work with. Oh yes, there were plenty. And I finally ended up with a team of five: Eric Davidson, Laurie Rowley, David Renwick, Andy Hamilton and Chris Miller.

A lunch was arranged with the producer, Keith Beckett. We hadn't met before, but we got along famously together. The enthusiasm was catching, and between us we'd jump from one idea to another. 'Oh, that'll be good', or 'How do you think this would work?'

Things gradually got under way: scripts were submitted, the wardrobe department came to discuss costumes, and the make-up department to see to wigs. It was all happening! I'd never experienced this sort of thing before – all these goings-on were centred around me. What did *I* think? What did *I* feel? In the past I'd been part of someone else's show – supporting them, and happy to do it. But now the limelight was on me, and I loved the warmth of it.

I came across the script of this first special the other day in my files. It looks as if every character we could think of was included. Mrs Thatcher of course, but also Barbara Cartland, Nana Mouskouri, Esther Rantzen, Elaine Stritch, Cleo Laine, Shirley Bassey, Hilda Ogden, Annie Walker, Barbara Castle, and many more. I still wonder at the number they managed to crowd into the programme.

Don Hunt was my musical director. I've learnt, if you ever work with a pianist – and this has happened many times to me in the past – who pops your music up in front of him, gives it a quick glance and says, 'Ah yes, that'll be all right,' then you're in for trouble. The really good ones never do this. They are as eager as you are to see that everything is spot on. 'Do you mind if we try that phrase again?' they'll say, or 'Let's just tidy that up a little bit there.' Don was one of the latter, conscientious and inventive. He helped and encouraged me enormously.

Rehearsals were great fun. Keith made them so, arriving with a scarf carelessly thrown over the shoulder, and lots of 'Darlings, let's try this' scattered about. He always achieved a gloss about his productions and I was delighted he was working with me. I remember there was a large set of steps I had to ascend and descend, rather like the kind of thing you see in a film musical where the dancers' heads suddenly appear over the top before they start walking down the other side.

'Keep your head up,' he shouted in the studio.

'I can't, Keith.' I've always disliked walking down stairs.

'Yes, you can. It will look a hundred per cent better. Go on, do it again.'

'I'm terrified I'll trip.'

'No you won't.'

And I didn't. And it did look a lot better.

He had a fine assistant in René Bloomstein. Quietly-spoken but highly efficient. I was accustomed from radio to marking my scripts, pencilling great cuts and putting huge arrows where to jump to next. It was fine by me, but not by René of the soft voice and firm manner. The script would disappear and yet another freshly-typed copy would be left on the table.

Everyone connected with the show wanted it to be a success. The clothes and wigs played a very important part. The research on this kind of thing is detailed. A photo of some style might be produced – 'No, it's not good, not recent enough. She's altered her hairstyle since then.' On the other hand, I found out from experience that people are slow to catch up with changes. Once an image is established that's the picture they retain. Take Esther Ranzten, for example: she had changed her style of evening gown from the off-one-shoulder type of thing to something quite different. But no matter, it was the off-one-shoulder look that registered as Esther, and I had to stay with it long after she'd moved on.

There's a great deal involved in putting the character together, discussing all the various points with make-up and wardrobe departments. I had several pictures of Esther to work from. It's usually helpful to have front face and profile. Her teeth – that was the first thing. I already had the set that was made for me for the Yarwood shows, but I went back to the dental specialist, complete with pictures, to have them re-checked. Every tooth had to be in exactly the same position as Esther's. The wig next: she had altered her hair – it was more blonde – but the rather casual style had remained. I looked again at the picture. On the day of the show it sits right there, on the make-up table in front of you. The mouth, the eyebrows, everything is important to arriving as near as possible to the real thing.

Her mannerisms: she is extremely feminine. At that time she had a way of sitting down in her swivel chair very slowly, crossing her leg over and smoothing her skirt before saying 'Good evening', the top lip trying its hardest to climb over the teeth, while her hand gently touched her shoulder. To me her voice sounds as if she starts at the top of a ladder and makes her way down.

My first meeting with her in real life had come about in a rather unusual way. I was sitting in my favourite little French restaurant, Le Provence in Kew – the owner, Jean, always makes you feel so welcome – when a little girl, walking rather unsteadily, came over to my table. She was holding a balloon attached to a string, and I could see she had no intention of being parted from it. I discovered her name was Emily, and as she chatted away, observing me with her large brown eyes, I heard a voice say, 'Sorry about that. But could I just say how much I enjoy your work?' It was Esther. She asked me if I would like to join them – them being her husband Desmond Wilcox and herself – as I was lunching on my own; and if I wasn't in too much of a hurry, then 'Why not come back to the house and have a coffee in the garden and put your feet up?'

It wasn't very long after Pete had died, and although nothing was said, I just got the feeling that they cared, and that this was their way of showing it. Since then they have become my friends. Desmond looks at me a little anxiously at times, and remarks, 'I don't think you really need to use the teeth.' And Esther tells him forcefully, 'Of course she does, mine are much bigger than hers.' And short of producing a measuring tape, I have to agree on that.

Included in the television special was an interviewing spot as Esther, meeting people such as Barbara Cartland, and Cilla, and so on, walking up to them in the street with the microphone and exclaiming: 'Good Lord. Look who's here! Excuse me, madam, but aren't you . . .' And on the final one, tracking a raincoated figure with her back to the camera, only to find when she turned around that it really was Esther! I asked if she would do this for me, and she replied, 'Of course I will, it'll be great fun,' and came down to the location the next day. When she arrived, complete wih Emily, she took one look at me and exclaimed, 'But you look more like me than I do.' I knew what she meant. She had come from a working day in the office, and I was basing my appearance on how she usually appeared on television.

'Hang on a minute,' I said, 'I'll try and get my hair altered to look more like yours.'

But at the same time, she was busy saying to the make-up girl, 'See if you can get my hair to look more like hers.'

I hope that when it was all sorted out the viewers got a good double – we certainly enjoyed ourselves! The only confusion was for Emily, looking at two mothers, dressed alike, hair, teeth, the lot.

From that time on we have remained friends, and I mean the kind of friends who say, 'Oh don't bother to ring, just stop by.' I do just that, and we have an evening of either fish and chips or Chinese. On one such occasion, we were in the middle of the meal when Esther suddenly said, 'Have you ever thought of doing an Edna Everage?'

'Yes, I have,' I said, 'but I can't get it.'

Then Esther went on, 'Well, actually, it's the only impression I can do.' And she proceeded to launch into a very good impression of Edna. 'Go on, try it.'

'I can't, Esther, I just can't get the pitch.'

'Of course you can. See, here. Pitch up, up, up.'

I tried.

'No, no, no, too low. Pitch a bit higher.'

I tried again my hardest, producing the most terrible sounds. I was no nearer sounding like Edna. But Esther did, along with a very satisfied smile. So if ever there's an impersonation competition in *That's Life*, I think Esther should do her Edna Everage impression. I've no doubt about it, she'll win.

Barbara Cartland was a challenge. I'm a size 10, so a special body had to be made. Eventually I ended up with a row of bodies on hangers which they kept in wardrobe for all the larger ladies in my repertoire. Everything about Barbara Cartland is pink and white and masses of jewellery. Platinum white hair, pink and white make-up, great thick black false eyelashes – described by Clive James as 'looking like two crows crashing into the White Cliffs of Dover'! She dresses in pink chiffon, and when photographed surrounds herself with pink azaleas. She talks quickly: 'Of course, my dear, the heroines of my books are all virgins' – she's got a thing about virgins. A wonderful character to impersonate.

When the scriptwriters first talked to me about doing a sketch as Barbara Woodhouse, I hadn't seen her because I'd been out of the country.

'Oh you must do one of her. She's the funniest thing on television.'

'Why, what does she do?' I asked.

'Well, she trains dogs, and she's serious about it. That's the funny part.'

I made a point of seeing her next television appearance. It was marvellous. Here was this woman pushing people about – 'Let me see how you're holding the lead. Not like that, not like that. Don't be so stupid, not like that. Like this' – and the poor individuals would be given a sharp push and their elbows would be straightened out, and then she would turn to the dog and in cooing tones say, 'And who's a lovely boy?' She obviously thought the animals were wonderful and their owners were idiots. It was great material, and I couldn't wait to have a go at it. The strong points, the things that came across to me on the screen, were her authority, her bossiness, and that kind of eager, almost sniffing-the-air look with her head pulled up as if she were trying to see over a hedge. All her expressions – 'Sit!' and 'Stay!' – that had become so well-known to the public, were an absolute godsend.

Barbara Woodhouse was the most difficult from a make-up point of view. The clothes were no problem, but getting the figure right certainly was – especially the top. She's much more well-endowed than I am, and I noticed that whenever she appeared in her skirt and navy sweater, walking along waving to the camera, everything underneath the sweater sort of – well, as Michael Parkinson said when he interviewed me, 'it wobbled'. I tried padded bras, but they didn't wobble. And then we got the idea of filling two balloons with water and popping them down a special little pocket made in the cups of the bra. That worked a treat.

On the day of filming everything was ready and, because we were on location and I was walking around, they fixed a little microphone down inside my blouse. Suddenly, in the middle of the scene, one of the sound boys came to me and said, 'We'll have to stop for a moment, Janet, we're having trouble picking up your dialogue.' When we checked the mike, they found it had slipped down inside the bra, and all it was picking up was the water slurping about in the balloons!

Because of the number of characters in my show, and their various make-ups, and because I was the only person appearing, it made everything a race against the clock to be back in front of the cameras as quickly as possible. Turning into Barbara Woodhouse from Sybil Fawlty, for instance, meant removing false nails, false lashes, a complicated wig firmly glued all around the hairline, and all the make-up and clothes; and then it was into all the padding for Barbara. This was followed by the bra, the heavy stockings, shoes, skirt and blouse, and finally the make-up. It took two make-up girls to apply the special glue around my eyes and mouth, and then two hairdryers going full blast on my face to dry it off. They pushed my skin into position to crease it and form all the fine wrinkles, while I sweltered underneath the heat of the dryer. But at the end of the day, if the result on the screen was good, everyone was delighted. It was all that really mattered, and worth every bit of discomfort.

Removing it all, I think, was even worse. My face was in and out of basins of hot water like a yo-yo, to soften the latex, and then came the painful process of pulling it off bit by bit. Many a time I said to the make-up girls, 'You have to love your work to put up with all this.'

Sometimes the changes were so fast, I had to dash out of the studio, throwing off a ring, a scarf, a wig, as I ran along the corridor to the make-up room, while the poor dresser hurried along behind catching all the bits and pieces.

It's a curious thing, but I have found that leaving one character behind and putting on another, I start to become her, using the voice of that person to answer someone instead of my own. I suppose it is warming up, in a way. If it was Barbara Woodhouse, then I would speak in her clipped tones, walk back to the studio muttering away as her, take my position in front of the cameras; and if there was a hold-up it was Barbara's voice that would say, 'Come along, come along, do get it right.' It's really very odd. I've said things to an audience I wouldn't dream of saying as myself. I can recall appearing in cabaret when a drunk, who had been making quite a nuisance of himself, suddenly shouted out to me in the middle of the Mrs Thatcher routine, 'Hey Maggie, what are you going to do about the family allowance?'

'Nothing,' I said, 'if it breeds people like you.'

Even now I go cold at the thought! It would never enter my head to make such a remark. For one thing, I wouldn't have the nerve. But when you're being the other person, then it's quite a different matter. Strange, isn't it?

When people ask how I practise an impression, I tell them,

'In the car, preferably when I'm driving home late at night.' It's the best place I know to go over a voice without feeling self-conscious. There have been moments, of course, when I have been practising them during the day. It's a very embarrassing thing to be deep in someone else's voice and facial mannerisms, only to find the person in the car next to you wondering what on earth you're up to. I've had this happen when I have been sitting at the lights pretending to be Cilla, busy with her 'Hello chucks, how are yer?' kind of thing, pushing the teeth well out – and then I've realized I am being watched. When that happens, I pretend I have something in my eye or my nose has an itch. After all, it's not the best expression to be caught out with in a traffic jam.

People often ask how I manage to look like the people I impersonate. It's an illusion created because you've caught something that's true. I don't try to analyse at all, something just clicks for me. I find a mental picture, and I cling to that. I believe Mike Yarwood tries things in the mirror. That doesn't work for me. I need to get within the character, then I proceed with what interests me in the voice. The mannerisms seem to follow through. I think if you really feel like the person then it will register on your face, and I think that is what the audience catch. All the time I'm doing the impersonation, that little mental picture of the real person is up there in front of me.

When the Television Special was completed – we had worked on it for two months – the studios gave a party for everyone connected with the production. In the corner of the room was a television set.

'Look at this, Janet,' Keith Beckett called. And up on the screen came the opening title, *Meet Janet Brown*, and the music. I felt butterflies in my tummy. We were all seeing the finished product for the first time: how the music sounded, how the clothes and make-up looked, how the sketches and dialogue had been tightened up, and what effects the cameras had achieved. It was one of the most exciting experiences I have ever had. For good or for bad, it was my show. Hooray! And hooray to everyone who had made it possible.

After the programme went out, my manager Bernard Lee rang me.

'Have you seen the figures?' he asked.

'What figures?'

'The ratings,' he said. 'It's number one in Scotland, and two in England.'

He was over the moon about it. When I heard the news, so was I. The critics were kind, and the result was a series in the autumn.

While all this was happening for me, Tyler and Emma were getting on with their lives too. Emma was studying in London, and Tyler had by now left Pangbourne College, a school he had loved. There would be no more mad drives to make it for Founder's Day, when all the families would be with their sons, and picnics were the order of the day.

I have vivid memories of one particular trip. My car had problems, and so, while they were repairing it, the garage in the next village gave me another to make do with. Emma and I collected it very early in the morning from where it had been left outside, and as we drove off I was horrified to see some dreadful stains inside that looked like blood to me. What was even worse, it had an evil smell, but there was no alternative. We loaded it up with all the picnic things, and set off. At the first set of lights I stopped, but the car didn't. Foot hard down on the brake, it made no difference. This happened the whole way, and by the time we reached Pangbourne, I was a nervous wreck. I was working in Eastbourne at the time and so I could only stay a little while and drive straight back. When I returned to the cottage I was exhausted. The strain of non-existent brakes had taken their toll. I could never have driven on to Eastbourne to do the show. But my good friend Helen Wise came to the rescue, took over the driving and I made it in time.

When I returned the car to the garage and told them in no uncertain terms about the state of it, they laughed.

'Notice a funny smell?' they said.

I certainly did.

'Belonged to a fishmonger,' they told me. 'Carried all the fish in it.' That explained the bloodstains!

The picture remains a very clear one – all those lovely cars, and us in a fish van next to them. No wonder Tyler felt as he did when we parked! Well, there are always excuses for people like us. I once took something to a Bring and Buy stall in the village, and as I left my offering on the table I overheard a woman say to her friend, 'What on earth is that?'

And the other replied, 'It is very odd, isn't it? But then it's been left by the Butterworths, they're theatre people, you know.'

Rehearsals began for my new series, *Janet and Company*. The scriptwriters suggested more new characters: Beryl Reid, Lorraine Chase, Sue Ellen. One of the problems of being an impersonator is finding fresh characters. Occasionally a person will suggest somebody to me, and I say, 'Have you any idea how they sound?' I have to be able to do the voice so that the character is instantly recognizable. It's no good if you have to start explaining to your audience. The public have got to know them right away. I remember doing an impersonation of Janet Street-Porter in London and the audience reacted immediately. I did it again only sixty miles away, and the audience just looked blankly at me. 'Have you any idea who I'm doing?' I asked. And they said, 'No.' At that time her programmes hadn't been networked. That's another thing you have to check.

Another thing I did – or thought I did – was a promotion for the Christmas show in my series, but before I describe that there's something I would like to put straight.

Lots of people don't believe that the programme *This Is Your Life* is really genuine. Well, it is. It really is a surprise. I know, for it happened to me. Earlier on, they had done Pete's life and I found the comparisons interesting. Here, before coming to me, is how it happened to Pete. They decided he should be 'caught' in Selfridges. The studio rang to talk to me about it, and to work out how they could get him there.

'How about a phone call from you saying you're buying a new dress, and you want him to come up and look at it before you make up your mind?'

'Don't be silly,' I said, 'he would think I was mental, he would never come up from Sussex just for that. But I tell you what might work – if you got Pinewood Studios to phone him, and say they had arranged for him to be photographed in one of the departments with some of the glamour girls for the next *Carry On* film, I think he might believe *that*.' And sure enough, he did.

But before all this took place, I had to get him away from home, so that I could find old diaries and addresses for the researchers. I didn't like this part: I felt awfully guilty looking at his personal papers.

On the morning of the programme I asked him where he was going to be that day, knowing full well he was going to be in Selfridges. But I feigned great surprise when he told me.

'Oh, really? Selfridges? I'm having my hair done nearby. Why don't I meet you?'

And so we arranged to see each other under the big clock outside. I was petrified. I felt so unnatural and nervous when we greeted each other. I was sure he would sense something. I looked at my watch – we shouldn't really be in the store until shortly after four. Everything was timed to the minute. But Pete was never one for hanging about, and he made it clear when I tried to stop him.

'Oh, I've just remembered – I need to buy some, er, toilet water. Yes, that's right . . .' I was in a real old state by now.

'Well, buy it,' he said. 'You don't need me for that.' And he strode off.

I ran after him in an absolute panic. It was terribly important he shouldn't be in the particular department where the cameras were until a certain time. Oh dear, I thought, as we approached the department, the cameras are trained on us, they're going to see us, we're supposed to be a happily married couple and here we are on the verge of a row.

Pete was met by the wardrobe mistress for the film. There were no girls to be seen. By this time he was decidedly edgy, and when he asked where they were, and she said they were changing, he walked off into the shoe department. Everything was going wrong. Suddenly through the tannoy system came an announcement. 'Would shoppers please wait a moment. The well-known actor Peter Butterworth is in the store, and he is in for a great surprise.' Eamonn Andrews's voice went on, 'If you can hear this, Peter Butterworth ...' Peter Butterworth couldn't hear it, he was in a department where the tannoy didn't reach!

Eamonn was hiding behind a clothes rack, microphone in hand and perspiration pouring down his face. He said later he aged ten years! Somehow I managed to get Pete to the spot where he should have been, and Eamonn duly surprised him.

The team had thought of everything when they planned this – except one thing. The human element. They assumed what Pete would do, and he had done quite the opposite. But in the end it was a lovely night for him. Many of his ex-Fleet Air Arm and prisoner-of-war friends turned up, Tyler and Emma were allowed out of school to be present, and I know that they felt very proud of him.

When it happened to me, the circumstances were completely different. I had gone along to Thames's studios at Euston to do the promotion for the Christmas show which I've already mentioned. Earlier in the day, I'd been lunching with Bernard, my manager, our yearly special lunch at Claridge's. The car was late picking me up to take me to the studio, and I rang to find out where it was. My secretary had said she knew I would do this – I never like being late for appointments. I found out later it was the old business of timing again, making sure I didn't arrive at the wrong moment, and bump into some of the guests. They had to be kept well out of sight.

When I got there they led me to a little studio where they were going to film the piece. It was to go out later in the month, they said. Of course, I believed it, why shouldn't I? The idea was for me to sit in the front row of an audience they had collected and I would watch the film clips go up, with me playing various characters, then turn to camera and say, 'These are some of the people you will be seeing in my show, so please look in at 10.30 tonight.' Where had the audience come from, I asked, as I looked round the little theatre. Oh, the office block, they're all office workers.

What fun! 'Hello, everybody. How are you? Have you all got Equity cards?' I was thoroughly enjoying the whole set-up. This should work very well, I thought. The lights went down, the film clips came on, and I saw myself playing several well-known stars. Then, suddenly, I was looking at a wig from the back. It was a bad one. What on earth had I been doing here, I wondered. That's a dreadful wig. How did I let that pass? Then the wig turned round, and it was Eamonn's face I was looking at. It still didn't register with me. What's he doing in my Christmas show? What's he doing in this bit of film? I heard his voice speaking to me, and then saying:

'. . . and if you look to your left, Janet . . .'

I did, and he was standing there, next to me.

How did I feel? A mixture of things, really. My immediate reaction was to think, 'This has got to be a joke – it must be.' And then, as it slowly dawned that it wasn't, I thought what an idiot I had been. I'd believed that all those people there were making up an audience, that what I had been doing was genuine, and I felt stupid. The next reaction was the awful realization, as Eamonn said the words, 'This is Your Life', that I was going to burst into tears. And when I saw the recording later, I noticed my hand had gone up to cover my face. My legs felt as if they had turned to jelly. It was a terrible fright and one I wouldn't like to experience again. Having said all that, I would also like to say it was one of the loveliest, happiest nights I've known.

After the initial surprise, I was taken to a hotel where I had time to get myself together before the actual recording. Thames wanted me to enjoy it. They saw how upset I was to begin with, and they said, 'Look Janet, we want you to have a marvellous night. You have nothing to do but sit back and enjoy yourself.' And I thought, right, I'll do just that. But when I walked through the audience my composure nearly left

1O DOWNING STREET

THE PRIME MINISTER

TO MISS JANET BROWN

I am delighted to send my good wishes to you today when your popularity and professionalism are recognised by 'This is Your Life'.

After many years as a versatile performer, your unique talent has brought you a well-deserved success. I compliment you on the accuracy of your impersonations - including those you do of me.

I can only imagine how many hours of hard work go into perfecting each little detail.

Your achievements and your popularity reflect two very important British characteristics - a sense of humour and the freedom in which to enjoy it.

My congratulations and best wishes for your continued success.

Margaret Thatcher

me. So many kind people were showing their affection, calling their hellos and patting me on the arm as I made my way to the stage, and I thought, I'm never going to make it. The whole thing had a feeling of unreality.

It began with Tyler and Emma coming on, smiling from ear to ear. How they managed to keep it a secret from me, I'll never know. Then out of the blue my sister appeared: they had flown her over from Canada. My brother was there, and many other friends. As well as family, there were so many of my TV friends from *Who Do You Do?* Goodness, what next? Here was Esther and her husband Desmond. Now what? I didn't have long to find out, for the brisk figure of Barbara Woodhouse marched in, complete with 'Walkies' written on her T-shirt. She practically took over the programme as she gave me a lesson in dog training. Carol Channing sent a message from New York. And Margaret Thatcher wrote me a lovely letter, which Eammon read out. The final surprise was the appearance of Jessie Matthews, the star who had been one of my first impressions and whom I had admired so much but never met. I had a great big lump in my throat at that moment. Oh, and I musn't forget the girls from the Co-op were there too!

Afterwards, when the programme was over, I went downstairs. To my surprise, my close friends Helen and Gerry Wise from Sussex walked in. 'How lovely to see you,' I said. 'Fancy coming up all this way to the studio.' I was delighted they were there to share this night with me. We had had so many good times together. Then behind them came two, then three more and gradually the whole room was full of my friends. There was a marvellous party. I loved it. The first party I've ever had especially for me. It was a great feeling.

Later on, I was given the big red book with my name on the cover and inside a set of pictures of everyone who had taken part in the programme. Also, in a black folder, a record of the whole show. Not only was it a complete surprise, it is still a lovely memory.

12

Janet and Company

Until I started writing this book, I had no idea I had jotted down so many bits and pieces in my diaries – things that have interested or amused me. Here's one: 'Jumped into a London taxi and the driver said, "Where to, Katie?" I said firmly, "It's not Katie." "Oh, so sorry," he said, "Lady Boyle."'

Here's another: 'Coming out of a fitting-room after trying on a dress and wandering round the department I saw a woman watching me; then she came towards me, and I thought: Here we go, an autograph hunter, and I reached into my bag for my pen. "Excuse me," she said, "but I think I ought to tell you you're wearing your cardigan inside out and your label's showing at the back."' In another store there's an elderly assistant who always grabs me by the arm and says, 'I've got it right today, it is Esther Rantzen, isn't it?' Then there's the couple who stopped me in the Isle of Wight – I was playing a summer season there. 'He is awful,' said his wife, 'but he wants to ask you something. Go on, ask her.' 'Well,' he said, 'are you the woman who works in the sweet shop at the end of the road?'

I see that after meeting David Attenborough at a television award luncheon, I wrote: 'David Attenborough says how marvellous I looked the other day in Marylebone High Street, wearing a very fetching poncho outfit.' It wasn't me, but I accepted the compliment! Princess Margaret at the same function talked about my impression of Mrs Thatcher. 'Dennis Thatcher says that if he closes his eyes he believes it's

181

Margaret.' She then added, 'What better accolade than that? It's the dewdrop on the rose.'

I've made a note, too, about a radio broadcast I was doing from Scotland and the young singer asking the producer very nervously, 'What did you think of that last song, was it all right?' And the producer replied, 'Oh aye, well, of the two, that one was the worst.'

Theatrical landlady stories are many, but this is one of my favourites. In Variety days, you could sometimes take food back to your landlady and ask her to cook it for you. This particular act left her some steak and asparagus to cook for their supper. On their return, after the show, the landlady greeted them cheerily with, 'Your steak is nearly ready and I've put your bluebells in a vase on the mantelpiece.'

During the troubles in Cyprus, when there were terrorist attacks on the British, I was on the island with Jimmy Edwards – we were doing shows for the Forces. One night, on our way back from a camp, a bomb was thrown at our bus. We all threw ourselves on the floor, and fortunately everyone was all right. But when the news came out in the papers at home – you know, 'Bomb Thrown at Artiste' – I received a telegram from Pete saying, 'Either change your act, or come home.'

Another entry makes me laugh. It was about our crazy way of living. We had both been working hard, he up early to film and me returning late from cabaret, so I used the spare bedroom and left him a note: 'Would you care to meet me in the lounge for coffee tomorrow morning? I shall be behind the third plant on the left.' The note on the table when I came down the next morning simply said in very large letters – 'YES! WHO ARE YOU?' He had such a lovely sense of humour.

Some people may think that I managed to deal with Pete's death fairly easily. Oh no. There have been many many times when I have been unexpectedly caught out. Driving along happily, the radio playing, and suddenly hearing 'Satin Doll', a jazz piece he loved. . . . Arriving at a theatre where we had both worked, and realizing as you look at the letter rack that there will never be another letter waiting. . . . Each time this sort of thing happens, you're never ready for it, and it's like being kicked in the stomach; you have to fight your way back, argue with yourself not to be silly when the tears come, and try and climb up again. I was in the middle of rehearsals one morning, singing and laughing, and a new actor had joined us. He lit up a cigarette – I didn't even notice – but the smell of it wafted across to me at the piano, and I found tears pouring down my face. It was terribly embarrassing, everyone thought someone had upset me. But they were the Gauloise that Pete always smoked and it reminded me forcibly of him. That's what I mean by saying it's when you least expect it. Happily, these moments have become rarer with time, while the affection and love we had for him remains.

Now, I haven't written this down so that you should feel sorry for me. Please don't, I'm a very happy, fortunate person. I've written it because there must be many like me who have gone through or are going through the same experience and I only want them to know that you *are* helped and strengthened when these times arrive, and you can find your way back. Love and warmth come from all directions. It's just being aware of this and being glad of it. And I hope by saying this, it helps someone.

When the next series started, Tyler was now deep in drama college and Emma had become a secretary at one of the drama academies. Tyler had tried out many jobs before deciding to become an actor. These had been varied, to say the least, and had included teaching, and even pig farming. He walked into the kitchen one day and said, 'There's a sweet little pig at the farm, it laughs every time it sees me,' and Emma replied, 'I'm not surprised.' That's sisterly love for you.

I asked her if she would like to be like Tyler and go to drama college. Her answer was short and to the point: 'No thank you, I don't want to pretend I'm a piece of toast.' So we dropped the subject!

There isn't any doubt in my mind that television work is some of the hardest work I've ever done. The days when we filmed the split-screen scenes were very long. Usually I was up at six, and down at the studio and in the make-up chair by seven. The make-up girl had often started earlier and had been up since five. When it was a character like Sue Ellen or Joan Collins, the make-up could last well over two hours. The split-screen – that's where you play more than one character and you talk to yourself, as it were, is difficult. It's complicated and tricky, and means trying to retain all the technical points in your mind while at the same time attempting to give a good impersonation of the character you're doing.

There was one lovely sketch, written by Chris Miller, called 'The Three Old Barbaras Locked in the Lavatory', and this consisted of the three Barbaras – Barbara Castle, Barbara Cartland and Barbara Woodhouse. The moves looked simple enough in the finished product. But simple they were not on the studio floor. I danced in and out of those loos all day long, and became utterly lost as to who I was supposed to be talking to. When I was Barbara Castle I had to face an imaginary Barbara Cartland, and so on . . . 'Where is she now?' I'd ask, as if it was someone else and not me that was playing it. 'Is my eye-line right, am I looking at the correct spot?' So many things to remember while Keith Beckett the producer darted from control room to the floor with endless notes. Usually this went on to ten-thirty, and sometimes beyond. I'd look over to my make-up girl and dresser, patiently waiting, their faces white with tiredness and yawning their heads off. But you can't do that when you're in front of the camera. The viewer must see it as if it is the very first time it has happened, and so you make yourself stay mentally and physically at that point of freshness and enthusiasm. Not an easy thing to do. When the floor manager shouted once again, 'Quiet please,' and then, stressing it, 'Let's *concentrate*,' I thought what a good word that is. And it was just what I needed to hear at that moment. I had been concentrating – you have to, otherwise you could be so easily distracted by the other things happening around you

– but having it underlined like that made me doubly conscious of what I was doing and I was most grateful to him for his conscientiousness. Each needs the help of the other. No one can do it all on their own. That goes all the way through the production, from the set designer to the boy who makes your cup of tea. We all need each other. When I was given three different awards for the series, everyone was delighted.

The Christmas show that year was great fun. It had my favourite sketch in it, the one with Rod Hull and Emu, and myself playing Mrs Woodhouse. I shall never forget the look on Emu's face when I said, 'At the count of ten I shall blow up his nose.' I counted slowly, 'One – two . . .' the bird meanwhile looking up with its evil face while it nodded its head at every number, and then as I reached ten, it dived at me. Its beak enveloped my face and I was forced back over the desk. The effect was hilarious. Although we had rehearsed the sketch endlessly, I could feel my heart beating like a hammer as I waited for the moment when the bird would swoop. It's extraordinary, isn't it? Here I am talking about it as if it really lives and breathes! It all goes to show how clever Rod Hull is: he can actually make you believe that it does.

I am frequently asked if the people I impersonate ever object. Well, I haven't found any that do. They all seem quite happy about it. From Mrs Thatcher all the way down the list. I remember reading an article about Janet Street-Porter saying she was so upset at my impersonation of her that she rushed upstairs and had a good cry. Well, that upset *me* so much, that I wrote a little note and sent her some flowers. It's never my intention to hurt anyone. I only want to share some honest-to-goodness fun with the audience. Naturally it means pinpointing the person's idiosyncrasies, but it is done without malice. In her letter back Janet thanked me for the flowers and said, 'Of course, we're all friends. Lots of love, Janet.' Later, when we met up in Australia, she generously supplied me with her own make-up and clothes and we did a double on television together. Every time I turned towards her, complete with teeth and glasses, she dissolved into laughter.

It's always interesting to meet the stars you impersonate.

Marlene Dietrich made a special impact. I saw her first of all at a midnight matinée at the Palladium in which all the other actresses had appeared in long evening dresses, and suddenly there was this wonderful vision in gold lamé – with a tight bodice and a short swirling skirt! She had very blonde hair and 'blazing' blue eyes. When she took her calls she bowed low, right down to the level of the stage and up, with her head thrown back . . . and those eyes! Suddenly you got the feeling that *she* was the show, everyone else was just there as an extra. The audience went wild, and I learnt another lesson in what it means to have 'star quality'.

When I went to Wolverhampton to do pantomime, and found she was doing her one-woman show at the theatre where we were going to appear, I just had to see her. The other members of the cast felt the same. Teddy Johnson and Pearl Carr, Jack Tripp, his partner Alan Christie and myself all dressed in our very best. The men wore evening suits and I put on a new and very lovely stage dress of the palest aquamarine lace, covered with tiny pale pink bugle beads, white fox furs and even a jewelled clip in my hair! Afterwards our producer took us backstage, saying, 'Marlene very much wants to meet my cast!' That made me laugh – I couldn't imagine *the* Marlene Dietrich requesting to meet us. I felt terribly nervous.

We went backstage. 'Miss Dietrich, I would like you to meet Miss Janet Brown.' She stood in her lovely pale pink lighting – how clever of her: normally the lights go out backstage at the end of a performance – a long cream-coloured coat over her sensational gold clinging dress. And the voice – that deep voice was saying, 'Oh, thank God you didn't come to the matinee. It was awful.' I don't know what I expected, but not that – not the thing we all say so often to friends, it was so stagey and pro-ey.

Searching for something to say, I stammered, 'What a lovely show, Miss Dietrich, and that orchestra! Could you leave it for our show!' And she replied, 'What about the dwess, darling, wouldn't you like the dwess?'

She held out her hand and took mine and didn't let go! I

wanted to stand back and take her all in. I was too close, but her face was beautiful, pale with a strong line of rouge on her cheek bones, and a great black curveline on the lids of those eyes. But it was her nose – it fascinated me. She had drawn a strong white line right down the centre. I know only that the next time I made myself up in the dressing-room, I did the same, and someone asked, 'What is that for?' and I said, 'I don't know; but if it's good enough for Marlene Dietrich, it's good enough for me.'

The second series of *Janet and Company* had us all racking our brains for more new characters. Dolly Parton and Shirley Williams were two of them. A foam rubber body was made for the Dolly Parton impression, and it reached from my neck to my ankles. Wardrobe made a great job of the outfit. Costumes of this kind always present a challenge. I felt as if I must have lost pounds, wearing it in the intense heat of the studio lights.

Shirley Williams was a very difficult one to get the hang of. I watched her on the news one night, walking along a station platform busily talking to some people, and a tune from the Mad Hatter's Tea Party came to mind – 'I'm late, I'm late, for a very important date . . .' Everything about her seemed to be hurrying and dashing – she had a kind of bundled look as if tied up with string. But it was only when I listened to her on a television interview that the feeling I was looking for came through. It struck me that the same kind of thing happened in her speech – a sort of rushing towards a word . . . and then leaping on it with great energy. She has a lovely voice – it's a very sexy one, I think. At that time she was in the news a lot, and I thought it wouldn't do any harm to have an impression of her ready, anyway, just in case Margaret Thatcher was out and Shirley Williams was in. It's as well to be prepared!

Sue Ellen from *Dallas* was an absolute gift. She had so many mannerisms – the wandering mouth, the anguished eyes, and of course the tears never far away.

We finished recording the series one afternoon. 'Is that it?'

asked Emma in surprise (she was acting as my secretary at the time).

'That's it,' I said.

'No parties? No farewells?'

'No,' I told her, 'the camera crew are probably going off to start on some other programme.'

It made me think back to the first television I ever did. The keyed-up feeling, the excitement, and then suddenly it was over. The lights dimmed in the studio, the cameramen left their cameras, and with a few casual 'Goodnights' everyone had gone. It was such an anti-climax. At least in live theatre the action is immediate. You know if the audience likes you or not. But with television so often you only really know how you've got on when some kind person in the street says, 'Saw you last night. You were great.'

When anyone says to me, 'You must get tired of that kind of thing?' I say, 'Oh no, never.' It's very comforting, and after all these are the people who go to make up your audience.

Talking of audiences, here's something I've never been able to work out. How is it that a theare can be filled with comparative strangers – they don't know each other, they're not talking to each other – and yet you'll hear artistes speak of a 'good audience' or a 'bad audience'? I've often wondered about this. How does this feeling generate itself, so that it presents itself to you on that stage with such solidness? It remains a mystery. If you the public could only hear how you're described sometimes – 'Weren't they a tough lot tonight?' 'What a ghastly crowd!' 'Weren't they a marvellous audience!' 'Aren't they terrific out there this evening!' I remember walking on stage one evening as another artiste was walking off. He muttered in my ear, 'I think this audience has been drinking cement!'

When I actually finished the series I felt absolutely drained. And so I got on a train the very next morning and went straight down to Cornwall. My neighbour has a studio flat there, facing the sea. It was wonderful. Only the beach, the seagulls and me. I shut the door on everything and just read and slept. I've learnt there has to be what I call a time for recharging the batteries, and when I left Cornwall I felt full of the joys of spring again. It's marvellous, isn't it, how you can feel quite worn out and then something just picks you up and revitalizes you. Jazz does that for me. Some of the pubs have smashing jazz groups and by the time I've had a cheerful earful of their playing I feel so happy I could take on the world. I think a pub lends itself to a much more informal and uninhibited atmosphere for jazz than does a concert hall.

Two of my favourite musicians are the great trombone player George Chisholm, and the legendary Stephane Grappelli. To hear George play 'Tea For Two' or 'Sweet Georgia Brown' transports you into another world. As for Stephane Grappelli, if you happen to be a fan of his you'll know what I mean, when I say that his playing describes for me more clearly than a dictionary ever could the meaning of the word 'joy'. It simply pours out of him.

The television series should have gone out at a regular time each week, but the Falklands crisis blew up, and there was no regular pattern. I watched Mrs Thatcher one evening on a television interview. There were two interviewers. She sat one side of the desk, they the other, both asking her penetrating questions. The hair was as immaculate as ever, so was the make-up. But as she replied to them, I noticed the perspiration making its way down the sides of her face, yet she never budged from her views. Instead she continually reminded them in adamant tones, 'Remember, we are not the aggressors.' I learnt later she'd been working flat out all day long and they expected her to cancel the interview. But she gave it, right on time.

Looking through my diary for 1982, I see that on 17 September I flew to Aberdeen to take part in the re-opening of His Majesty's Theatre, and in brackets I've written 'Very funny speech by Prince Charles'. As always on those occasions when royalty is present, there was an enormous amount of detailed rehearsal beforehand. During a quiet moment, I took myself way up into the gods and looked down to the circle and the stalls below. It really was beautiful. I remember thinking, 'It's like a big iced cake, with its cream tiers and designs picked out in gold leaf.' In the centre, hanging from the high ceiling, was a magnificent crystal chandelier holding court over all. The proscenium arch was of marble, and with the glow of the red velvet seats the overall effect was one of immense style and beauty. I knew a lot of money had been spent to bring the theatre back to its former glory, and I felt sure no one could possibly be disappointed with the result.

After the performance on the opening night, the curtain remained up while Prince Charles made his way round to meet the artistes on stage. Later on I was told by the director of the theatre, James Donald, that the Prince had turned to him and very unassumingly had said, 'Of course, you won't want me to say anything,' and James had replied that they would be delighted if he would say a few words. He then walked on stage and gave a most amusing speech. It was completely off the cuff and included references to items in the show, all done with great humour. The Provost, who was a small man, introduced him, and as Prince Charles stepped forward to the microphone, which was a riser – that is, coming straight up from the stage itself – he said, 'Well, at least I'm faring better than the previous act' – meaning the Provost – 'at least the mike is the right height for me.' And then he added, 'What you can't see and I can, is that down there' – and he pointed in the hole in the stage where the mike came up – 'is a little man raising the mike up and down.' There was a slight pause, and then with such lovely timing he remarked, 'Come to think of it, I'd better watch where I stand.' And he stepped back slightly. The laugh that followed would have gladdened any comedian's heart. The reason for it? He was wearing the kilt!

There is no doubt that Scottish audiences have a very special affection for the Royal Family, and on a night of this kind you can feel the warmth and the homeliness that I don't think you would find anywhere else. The Prince obviously enjoyed himself, and he talked with everyone on stage. One thing about this remains strongly in my mind. I had the same feeling when the Queen spoke to me at the Royal Command Performance. They have this ability to talk with others without giving out too much of themselves. It's a great art. I could do with a few lessons. I'm inclined to give out too much, and after an interview with a journalist I'm often quite exhausted. Now, the difference where they are concerned is that they pace themselves. They make conversation, they laugh, but always there is this relaxed holding back. I've come to the conclusion that this must be absolutely necessary, otherwise I don't think they would ever last the day.

I had eight very happy days in Aberdeen. What a lovely city it is. The weather was kind, even good enough to sit on the beach, and my hotel was friendly and enjoyable. One night at dinner one of the diners, came reeling over to my table. I had just popped a piece of steak into my mouth when he fell upon me. 'Come on, come on. Gie us yer Maggie Thatcher,' he said in the lovely Aberdonian accent.

'I'm sorry, but I'm eating.'

'Aye, aye,' he repeated, prodding my arm as if I'd never spoken. 'Gie's yer Maggie Thatcher, come on.'

So I swallowed the steak down, and in very cold tones I informed him, 'I'm going to shake hands with you, and then you're going to go straight back to your table, sit down, and I don't want to see you for the rest of the evening. Do you understand?'

'Aye, great, great!' he replied, and reeled back across the room, not the least bit offended.

Tyler was in rep in Dundee and I said I'd call in and see him on my way back. The train took me along the coastline. Oh, how beautiful Scotland is. I have a dreadful conscience about how little I know of my native country, but I comfort myself by continually saying, 'Never mind, one of these days . . .'

Emma was twenty-one that December. It's tough when your birthday is so near to Christmas. She'd made no special requests, and I wondered what would be a lovely surprise. A small dinner party for her friends was arranged for the evening, but what would be really special?

'How about this, Emma,' I said. 'I've booked you in at a hotel in London for the night, and I've arranged for a car, complete with chauffeur, to pick you up the next morning and take you wherever you wish to go around town.'

She was thrilled to bits. 'Will he walk behind me carrying parcels, the way they do in films?'

'I don't see why not.'

She and her girlfriend had a great day. The chauffeur, I was told later on, had started off very grandly, asking in the politest of tones, 'Where to, Modom?' But by the end of the day the mantle had slipped, and it was good old cockney 'Well, girls? Where d'you wanna make for now?'

I've worked in some weird and wonderful places, but surely one of the strangest has to be an appearance at Madame Tussaud's. I was giving a cabaret at a private dinner party. It really was extraordinary. What a star-studded audience I had – President Sadat, Ghandi, and Mrs Thatcher staring at me from behind her desk, her pen poised as if to write me a stiff note. I was slightly put out when I noticed that all the Royal Family seemed to have better lighting than myself. They stood at the back of the room, their faces showing no interest whatsoever. It was wonderfully funny, and I thoroughly enjoyed calling out to them, 'Can you hear me at the back?' I said to the guests at the tables, 'I'll know that those of you who don't applaud must be dummies.'

That same week I took part in Denis Norden's television programme, *Looks Familiar*. His visiting guest artiste was Alice Faye. What an unassuming person. One of her friends whispered to me as we watched her, 'She hasn't been able to sleep all night, she's so nervous about doing this show.' It's hard to believe, isn't it, that an actress who has starred in so many big Hollywood musicals should feel like this. I find it kind of comforting in away, to realize that – even when you are as big as that – you still have the old butterflies.

13

The Falklands Pilgrimage

I was at home in Sussex one day when the phone rang. It was a call from Derek Agutter, the head of CSE – Combined Services Entertainment. He said he wanted to send a party of artistes to the Falklands, but with a difference. It was to accompany the families who were going out to visit the war graves, and he was keen for me to go. It would mean a sixteen-hour flight to Montevideo, then three days at sea going down to the Falkland Islands. During that time, the families on board were to be entertained.

'Derek, can we do as many shows as possible in the Falklands for all the boys there?' I asked.

'That's exactly what I want,' Derek replied.

And so a letter duly arrived, phrased in Army-like terms. I was to 'report' to the Cunard Hotel in London at '1630 hours' on the evening of 4 April 1983, to meet the others in the party, and to be given all the details of the pilgrimage.

The Cunard Hotel is enormous, and when I arrived it was milling with people and lots of little children running around. Messages kept coming continuously over the tannoy. The whole place was a hive of activity. I was introduced to our tour manager, Phillip Jay – a splendid man, who from the beginning to the end of the trip looked after his party like a mother hen with her brood.

At the Cunard I also met the other artistes in the cast – comedian Ken Goodwin, the singer Jan Messender, Tommy Vance, the radio disc jockey, Lips, the singing duo, Bob Carolgees and Spit, and the mind reader Nigel Ellery. Our musical director was Maurice Merry.

The call for the next morning was at five o'clock. Ghastly hour! And it was only as we prepared to leave – coaches were taking five hundred of us to the airport – that the realization of what this trip was really all about hit me. Families were standing in line waiting for their call to the coach. Many held wreaths. I looked at them, and at the people holding them, and felt suddenly overwhelmed.

Before we left we were asked questions by the press. An interviewer from the BBC asked, 'Don't you feel rather strange about entertaining families on the ship under such difficult circumstances, and how will people feel about being entertained?' I could only say that there was no way of knowing how people would react, but I felt that those who wanted to, would come to the show; and those who felt otherwise would stay in their cabins. I needn't have worried about anything, for like all the other artistes I'd been very apprehensive. The people themselves told us how they felt about it, and I was warmed by their remarks.

'Oh Janet, it's nice to see you with us. Just give us a laugh, won't you.'

Others came up and said, 'Will you be giving us your Mrs Thatcher?'

'Of course I will,' I told them. I knew it could perhaps be a sensitive point with some of the families, but after all it is the impersonation most associated with me. And I was delighted that there was great applause at the first show when I finally ended my act as Maggie.

As far as the boys in the Falklands were concerned, she was the tops, and the cheers that greeted the impression of her nearly took the roof off. Nowhere can you get a more wonderful welcome than from a Forces audience. We gave three shows that day at the Town Hall, Port Stanley – 2.30, 5.30 and 8.30 – and at each one the place was bursting at the seams. Like the people on the ship, they just wanted a good laugh.

The flight to Montevideo was marvellous. A British Airways crew had volunteered and given their services free. They simply wanted to help. We were all aware of their kindness and thoughtfulness; nothing was too much trouble. Although at the Cunard Hotel everyone had been complete strangers, the flight changed all that. Families got talking, children ran up and down the aisle happily chatting to everybody, and many people found they had a link with someone because their sons or husbands had served together. I sat with Ken Goodwin, and we laughed and talked throughout the flight. I discovered he was as bad as I was at fixing headphones to listen to the radio, or finding the right button to tune in to the film – absolutely hopeless! I said, 'If anyone is looking over at all this performance going on, the reading lights above suddenly beaming down, the stewardess being buzzed by mistake, the wires of my radio under your behind, they'll think we're in our dotage!' The laughs made the flight seem much less than sixteen hours; he was great company, and one of the nicest people you could ever meet.

It was eleven in the evening when we arrived at Montevideo, and eleven coaches stood on the tarmac to take us to the dock where the Cunard ship the *Countess* was waiting. We left the aircraft quickly and without any fuss, watched only by cameramen, the quietness of the night broken only by the sounds of flashing light bulbs and the odd words from the soldiers who stood at the bottom of the aircraft steps, rifles in hand. I think most of us felt slightly uneasy, and were relieved when we reached the ship.

After I had found my way to my cabin and generally got myself organized, it was lovely to snuggle down in my bunk, and to feel the ship gently easing away from the dockside around four in the morning. The three-day journey to the Falklands and back is one I will always remember. Contrary to what we were told about the weather, the sun shone, and everyone found their way to the upper deck to lie back and lap up the warmth. It was nice to know the anorak and thermal underwear could stay in the case!

In some respects it was easy to be lulled by the surroundings into almost believing this was just another cruise ship. But the messages over the tannoy reminded us of why we were on this voyage.

'Will those collecting floral tributes for *HMS Coventry* please go to A Deck . . .'

There was such a cold feeling in my stomach as I listened to those messages. Everything seemed to stop for a second – breath, movement – followed once more by this overwhelming feeling of sadness.

During the time the ship was making its way to the islands, we were to hear this type of message many times. Wherever one of Her Majesty's ships had gone down, then our ship sailed to that spot, and a service was held for all those who had been lost.

Because the *Countess* had been requisitioned as a troop ship, a flight deck had been built to enable aircraft to land. The burial services were conducted on that deck, but I never went to any of them. I couldn't. They were so deep and personal, and I felt they were really only for the families concerned. But members of the Forces on board were full of compassion, giving comfort and care wherever they could. And it was not an unusual sight to see a soldier or a Wren with an arm round some grieving relative.

What struck me originally on this voyage was the absence of uniforms on the ship. Then, suddenly, rather like a Bond film, everything changed. I entered the dining-room one morning to find that the quiet retiring man I had been chatting to at my table was a Colonel, and there he was – pips and all. Another was wearing his navy blue naval Guernsey, tabs on his shoulders. When I asked how this turn of events had come about, I was told we had now entered British waters. Before that, the Forces on board had kept a very low profile. They didn't want to draw any more attention to the ship than was necessary. An officer said to me, 'I thought the families might be upset to see so many in uniform.' No such thing! One mother remarked to me, 'Don't our boys look fine in their uniform? It makes me feel so secure to see them.'

I was rather dreading my first sight of the Falklands, probably because of the number of times I'd been told how bleak they were. I wondered how this would affect all those families who were going to see the land that their sons and

husbands had fought for. But the weather stayed unbelieve-
ably good and I found myself looking at these gentle islands,
which seemed to me to have a great peace about them, with a
feeling of surprise and relief. Many others voiced the same
thought. The air was so pure, and the skies in the evening
were beautiful.

We anchored in San Carlos Waters, and then our party
prepared to go ashore to give the first show for the troops on
the island. On went the anorak and wellies and up we went to
the flight deck to wait for the Sea King helicopter that was to
take us to Kelly's Garden. It was my first experience of flying
in a helicopter, all very noisy, but highly exhilarating!

Kelly's Garden had such a romantic sound to me – it
conjured up visions of candle-lit tables under the trees. You
should see it! We were lucky the weather had remained good.
I was told the camp had been a sea of mud a short time before.
It was all Army huts, but they had made a make-shift theatre
by fitting several Portakabins together. When we arrived, we
were told how the boys had picked the names out of a hat to
see who would be the lucky ones, and that many would not
have the chance to see the show. I had a quick word with our
manager Phillip Jay and a chat with Ken and the others. 'Why
can't we adjust the times, then we could get two shows in?'
Everybody was more than happy to do this, so that was it
settled. I tell you, you have more fun at times like these than
you could possibly have at the Palladium. We only had an
Army blanket slung up as a kind of dividing line between us –
I mean between the girls in the company and the boys. We had
a trestle table to put our make-up on, but no lighting, and
when I asked where the plug for the hairdryer was I was
informed it was in the ceiling of the Portakabin. Oh, well, that
was no problem. I just stood on a chair to do my hair. The
stage was constructed of some boards held together with a
form of sacking on top. But it was all that we needed. With a
roll of the drums and a sweeping arpeggio from the piano we
were off. Marvellous. Great cheers from everybody, and two
highly satisfied audiences. We returned to the ship feeling
more than rewarded by the reception we'd been given.

There is one thing I would like to make clear about this ship. The *Countess* wasn't a sad ship. People wanted to live their lives as normally as possible, and so although at home you possibly saw on television only the very sad moments, there was lots of fun as well. Dancing, bingo, disco, treasure hunts for the children and fancy dress competitions. I know our show also helped a great deal to lift people's spirits, and for one rare moment in my life, I saw that if there was any real value to our work as artistes, then surely this was where it had its true meaning. Ours is a wonderful profession, I think, in that it provides opportunities to experience moments such as these.

Although our concerts were for the relatives of the servicemen, we didn't forget the crew – they needed to laugh as well. They were not allowed in the cabaret room, but we all went down to the Pig – that's the crew's own bar – and gave a performance just for them. What a great night that was! You could hardly see across the room for smoke, and the heat was stifling. But their enthusiasm made up for everything, and we would gladly have done the whole show all over again.

We continued to give our performances ashore to the Navy, the Army and the Air Force, sometimes splitting our party in two to cover as many bases as possible, and performing three times in the day wherever we could. In the short time we were there we gave ten shows. We had some great laughs. Trying to get everything on the back of an Army truck in the dark is no mean feat. We ended up sitting on drum kits, on guitar cases – shades of my Army days – and it was just as well we couldn't see where we were going as we bumped and thumped and swayed over the terribly uneven ground. There were screams of laughter as we fell all over the place, desperately holding on to the sound equipment and convinced that at any second someone would disappear over the side. All this was followed by trying to jump into a small motorboat, again in total darkness. I was given my instructions: 'Hold my hand. Now move over to the left – watch it – no, not there, you'll fall in – right, jump!'

We finally arrived back at the ship well after two in the

morning, tired but happy that everything had gone so well.

The next day two jerry cans of water were delivered on board – a 'thank you' from the Army. The water on the ship was really awful and when Margaret Thatcher had phoned from England to enquire whether everything was satisfactory she had been told that the only complaint was about the bad tea!

Here are some of the notes I made in my diary:

SATURDAY 9 APRIL 1983
A strange unreal day. At 11 am we rendezvoused with *HMS Cardiff* on the site where *HMS Coventry* went down. From 12 noon services were held on the Flight Deck. I feel I can't intrude. So many grieving families. Personnel from the services and officers from ships who saw action were torn apart by it all. All these families have their own personal reason for being there and who can blame or decide what is right for anyone. For some it is sailing to the spot where the ship went down and holding a proper service; others just have to see what had been fought for. Sir Rex Hunt on board from helicopter. Invitations for all the families from all the Islanders. It's listening to the ordinary things that get you. There was a mother who had been given a piece of rock from Bluff Cove – 'This officer who brought it called at the house. He was very kind, and helped with the washing up at the funeral.' Such everyday talk, and so heart-breaking. I'm just so glad to be on this trip. To have families thank us for the show and tell us how it lifted their morale is lovely to hear.

SUNDAY 10 APRIL
The dedication service was held this morning at San Carlos. To begin with I felt it would be an intrusion to be there and the night before said I would certainly not be going. But when the morning came my thinking had changed. I just wanted to be there and I found most of the others in the party felt the same. There were launches to take us to the land, each group leaving when its launch number was called

– all so well organized. It's a short walk up the hill to the cemetery. We had been told to wear our wellies, and I was glad of them. The cemetery had a simple brick wall almost circular in shape and around it stood the people. Just standing, silent, waiting. Inside the wall were the graves and simple headstones. Flowers were already lying on the graves from the families who had gone the day before to hold their private service. A helicopter circled and landed, and the VIPs arrived, among them Sir Rex Hunt, Governor of the Islands. Then the service began. I found it awfully hard to keep back the tears. Everything was so still, the sun breaking through while people stood silently, holding their own personal wreaths, sprays of flowers, crosses of poppies. Mothers, fathers, wives, children. The hardest moment, for me anyway, was the piper's lament and the steady walking forward of the various Services with their wreaths – placing them and saluting. Then the people following with their own tributes.

I looked over to one woman who had been fairly emotional on the voyage: now she stood, composed and erect, singing the hymns. And the young Naval Officer's wife, holding one single white rose – my heart went out to her, she was so very brave.

Returning on the little boat after the service I thought again of the stillness – the single sound of a cock crowing, somewhere a baby crying – as everyone stood motionless. One girl on the ship had laughed with me about her 'daft' husband – he had been with the SAS. 'He loved to lie on the floor, the children crawling all over him.' She felt she just had to see what he had been fighting for. Now she sat in the launch taking us back to the ship, her face crushed with grief. You could only try and support her with your thoughts. She had told me, 'He'd be away for five months at a time – I was used to him not being around.' But she added, 'We had to go to their aid – after all, they're British.' Now it was registering that this time he wouldn't be coming back. She was wonderful, though. The next night on the ship there she was – a big bright smile on her face. 'It's time

I got home, I'm not used to having free time like this all
day. I've lost nearly a stone, I think – all the strain. I'm
smoking myself to death! . . . I'm used to being up at 6,
washing the baby's nappies, seeing the children off to
school.' (She had three children.) 'No, I can't be doing with
this – too much time on my hands.' And off she went, still
with that big wide warm smile. A smashing girl.

MONDAY 11 APRIL

A most moving sight. The ships *Cardiff* and *Active* pass the
Countess in silent tribute – all sailors standing rigidly along
the decks, hands on rails, rows of white sailor's caps. All
officers at attention and, on the upper deck, the lone figure
of the Captain, standing motionless, silhouetted against the
sky. So beautifully done. Families were deeply touched and
fiercely proud of being British.

TUESDAY 12 APRIL

Sent cards home to all who asked for Falklands stamp. The
skies are so lovely. Tonight met Major-General David
Thorne, the Commander of the Forces, and Sir Rex Hunt
on the bridge of the *Countess*. In his message to everyone
aboard the General said that all that had been done for
everyone while on the ship was 'an act of love'.

At 5.30 there is a Harrier jets fly-past, and then the
Cardiff and *Active* go past at speed, this time in cheering
tribute, white caps in the evening light – three cheers – then
an abandoned mad cheering and whistling – all along the
decks, placards, waving, messages being shouted, really
marvellous. 'Only the British could do this,' the families
say.

Looking back on this period, I think of the feeling of the
Falklands Pilgrimage. To me it was a great feeling of love, and
concern, one for the other. It is truly an experience that I shall
always remember and I'm grateful to have met and shared this
experience with such fine people.

14

'Can We Talk?'

Before starting out on the Falklands Pilgrimage, I had written to Mrs Thatcher. In my letter I said: 'I'm off to the Falklands and naturally I'm taking you with me.' When I returned, there was a letter from Number Ten waiting for me. 'Let me know as soon as you return,' she wrote, 'and come and have lunch at Chequers.' I immediately rang her secretary.

'Well, we've seen what she's written to you,' she said, 'but she doesn't seem to realize what a full diary she has. And with the run-up to the election, I'm afraid it's impossible at present.'

Naturally I was disappointed when I heard this, but I thought, well, at least I can thank her for her invitation. And so I wrote, saying how sorry I was because there was so much I wanted to tell her about the Falklands while it was still fresh in my mind. But that I quite understood how busy she must be. The next day I received a call from Number Ten. Could I make it for tea at Chequers this coming Sunday? Of course I could, but after all it was Mrs Thatcher's only day off. Wouldn't she rather leave it until later?

'Oh no,' the secretary answered, 'she's very keen that you should come.'

And so on the Sunday I set off in my car, complete with the little map that had been sent to help me find my way there. I just assumed I'd see lots of security when I arrived, but I didn't. It looked peaceful and quiet, and following the instructions I made my way in by the side entrance. There were two policemen on duty, the only two I saw. They must press a little bell or something, for as I drove into the courtyard, Mrs Thatcher was making her way down the steps to greet me. I thought that was nice. It took away that rather awful thing of entering a strange room for the first time. It was a friendly sitting-room that we went into, with a log fire burning away in the fireplace. And there was only a friend there, and Mrs Thatcher and her husband Denis. I liked him a lot, he was very easy to talk to. Mrs Thatcher was rather quiet, and I wondered if Sunday was *her* day for recharging the batteries.

While we were talking, the door opened and a Woman Police Officer entered, carrying a large tray with afternoon tea. I wanted to laugh. It was like a scene from the play *Anyone for Denis*.

I don't quite remember how I got into the following dialogue – probably it was something to do with seeing the tray laden with sandwiches and cakes – but anyway, I was off.

'I had friends to tea yesterday, Mrs Thatcher, and I decided I would give them a real English tea. You know, muffins, Chelsea buns, maids of honour . . '

'Maids of honour?' said Mrs Thatcher. 'Are they the little sponge cakes with the cream and two little bits on top?'

'No, no, those are butterfly cakes. No, I mean maids of honour, that are made especially at the Maids of Honour Tearoom in Kew. They're famous, you know, for these cakes. Well, I had these . . .' and I rambled on. Mrs Thatcher rose swiftly to her feet and with great concern said, 'Oh, do please eat something, it's all for you.' I suddenly realized it must have sounded as if my tea was better than hers. But it was too late, I was well in with both feet now. It was only driving back that I saw the funny side of it and burst out laughing.

I spent a lovely afternoon with them both. She was quite anxious about me, saying, 'There's not much of you, you know. You're not dieting, are you?' as she passed me the sandwiches. At five o'clock I said, 'I really must go. You must have some time to yourself.' But she replied, 'You've come all this way to see me, wouldn't you like to see round Chequers?' I was only too delighted and found it charming and interesting. As she showed me round she explained the paintings, talked about the pieces of furniture and how she'd moved some of them around so that they could be seen better, and finally asked me to sign the visitors' book. I felt very honoured.

'Now, I really must go, Mrs Thatcher, and let you have a little of your Sunday.'

But Denis wouldn't hear of it. 'Come along, you'll have a bite of gin, won't you?'

'I don't know about a bite of gin, but I'd love a bite of Perrier water.'

When I left they came to the door with me, and I turned to wave to them at the corner, the way I always do to my family. And that's the picture that remained with me, the two of them at the door, waving to me until I was out of sight. Yes, I had a really marvellous day!

Perhaps the most fun I've had pretending to be the Prime Minister has got to be the visit to Los Angeles and my meeting with the American comedienne Joan Rivers.

I had an unexpected call one evening from Digby Wolfe, the very fine comedian who left England and become a writer for American television shows, including the *Laugh-in* show. He was phoning me from his home in Beverly Hills. I hadn't heard from him in years. 'Go on, you're at Haywards Heath station, you're much too clear.' But he wasn't, and he quickly put me in the picture as to why he was phoning. He had come up with an idea to play a hoax on Joan Rivers, and fool her into believing I was Margaret Thatcher. It was to be filmed for television, a kind of 'candid camera' idea, and it was being set up by Johnny Carson. It appealed to my sense of humour, and before I knew what was happening, I was in Los Angeles.

A meeting was arranged with the director and producer. 'Here's what we want you to do,' they explained. 'Johnny Carson has invited Joan Rivers to a private dinner in Las Vegas, and she's agreed to go. He had made his private jet available for her and it will be waiting at the airport. When

Joan Rivers arrives at the TWA desk, she'll be told there's a hold-up because Mrs Thatcher is on her way through and so she might have to wait a little in the VIP room. And that possibly Mrs Thatcher might use the room as well. If so, they would try and arrange an introduction.'

I listened to everything, and then explained that as Joan Rivers hadn't at as yet appeared in England, I didn't know what she looked like. They were surprised at this, but arranged for me to see some of her tapes. It was quite an experience. I'd never seen anyone like her. Her delivery is fast and attacking. I thought she was very funny. She had a catch phrase – 'Can we talk here, can we talk?' And her jokes on the Royal Family were really something.

'Now here's what we want you to do,' the director explained. 'We want you to be introduced to her, and we want you to be charming to her for about ten minutes, then really go to town and tell her exactly what you think about her remarks on the Royal Family. You know the kind of thing,' the director said, 'really build it up. Say, um, "England might go to war over it" or something.' I felt I could hardly say *that*, but I knew what he meant.

The day before all this took place I was taken to see the VIP room they were building at the airport. It looked a shambles. The ceiling was ripped open, new lights were being installed, and behind the fake mirrors and pictures they'd place hidden cameras.

'We've put microphones into the plant pots,' they told me, 'in case you have to walk around, and they'll pick up the dialogue.'

Now actually, there was no dialogue written for me, there couldn't be. For one thing, I didn't know how she'd react, what she would say, or whether she would blow her top and walk out of the room. It all had to be played by ear.

The next day I was driven to the airport in the biggest car I've ever been in in my life, complete with dark windows and a cocktail cabinet. I was wearing the navy blue suit, the blouse with the pie-frill neckline, and my hair was immaculate. I was shown into an ante-room.

'She's arrived,' they said, meaning Joan Rivers, 'and she's gone up to the VIP room. We'll give her ten minutes, then in you go.'

I should tell you that all the cameramen were in black trousers and black T-shirts, completely out of sight, of course, and there was a hidden control panel. Around sixty people were involved in the set-up.

'Right,' the director said, white with nerves and looking at his watch, 'in you go.' And then he added, 'And for God's sake don't screw it.'

I couldn't believe it! 'What a silly thing to say,' I told him. 'You remind me of a producer I once worked with in England. We were just about to start the scene in the studio and he said, "Don't forget the words."' Obviously I was going to do my best.

They had arranged it all brilliantly. As I walked along the corridor there were six security men around me. They had the press, television interviewers with their microphones pushed up against my face and camera lights flashing. Joan Rivers had walked past all this and had accepted it was for Mrs Thatcher's arrival. I took a deep breath, and entered the room, surrounded by my bodyguards. We stood for a moment in a corner, and then someone approached me.

'I wonder, Mrs Thatcher, if you'd be good enough to come and meet one of our foremost American comediennes, Joan Rivers.'

'Certainly,' I replied graciously, and proceeded to cross the room.

'Mrs Thatcher, may I introduce Miss Joan Rivers . . .'

As I shook hands and said, 'How do you do?' she started, 'How do you do, Mrs Thatcher, this is my husband Edgar, my manager . . .'

'How do you do, how do you do. My, you certainly travel with a great many people, don't you?'

Before going into the room the director had instructed me: 'If her husband goes to sit down next to her, move him. I don't care how you do it, just move him. We must have the two of you together for our camera shots.'

Sure enough, Edgar moved to sit down.

'May I,' I leapt in quickly, 'sit next to your charming wife?'

Outwardly, I had Mrs Thatcher's iron calm, but inwardly I was as taut as a violin string. We got under way with our conversation. All the time I was looking into Joan Rivers' eyes, I was thinking, 'She can't *really* be believing this?' But she was. Completely. She was on the edge of her seat – 'Yes, Mrs Thatcher . . . No, Mrs Thatcher . . . ' – where was this volatile lady I'd watched? I could feel my mouth getting drier. How on earth was I going to attack someone who was being so polite? Right, I thought, here we go.

'Miss Rivers, one of my aides was kind enough to let me hear some of your material on our Royal Family, and I must say I found it absolutely *disgusting*.'

Her face was a study. 'Oh, well, just call me a court jester, Mrs Thatcher, call me a court jester,' she laughed nervously.

I pounded on. 'And your remarks on Princess Anne. Well, of course, I've spoken to President Reagan and, as you know, we've been friends for years . . . '

She was in a high old state by now, and suddenly burst out with: 'I hate to remind you, Mrs Thatcher, we fought for you, but we fought for you . . . '

Somewhere in her material I remembered her saying, 'You don't know what the English are talking about when they speak, they go "Fah fah, fah fah . . . ".'

I heard myself saying, 'I've been told you have great difficulty understanding English people, and when they speak they go "Fah fah, fah fah". Can you understand what *I'm* saying?' My tone couldn't have been more grandly condescending.

'Oh *perfectly*, Mrs Thatcher, *perfectly*.'

It was time for the final piece. 'I don't think you *really* understand what I'm saying, and so I want you to read this letter . . . '

I took out of my bag a letter from Johnny Carson.

'What, now? Read it now?' And she fished for her glasses.

The note said: 'Dear Joanie, this is just a joke. And we hope you take it as such. If you don't, we don't care a . . . '

There was absolute silence for a second. Then she threw back her head and roared with laughter. I thought she was wonderful about it.

'But if I'm not talking to Mrs Thatcher, who are you, for heaven's sake?'

When I told her, she answered, still laughing, 'Well, who's going to know it's not Mrs Thatcher? Come on, let's have our pictures taken together. I want it for the top of my piano!'

On the flight back, my manager, Bernard, and I chatted about it. 'I doubt if she'll ever let that be shown on TV. It makes her look a fool.'

But I disagreed. 'I think she'd be mad not to let it be seen. After all, it lets the public see what a good sport she is.'

In the event, it not only went out once on American television, it went out three times, and I gather Joan's words were: 'If you dish it out, you have to be prepared to take it.'

This job of mine has taken me all over the place, and has given me a great deal of happiness and many friends. When I first started thinking of a title for the book, Tyler said, 'Why don't you call it *There and Pack Again*?' Actually, that sums it up rather well, for I seem to have spent an awful lot of my life doing just that. In fact I've just returned from a tour of Australia. But one thing I'd never tackled is giving an impression of a writer. Well, I've had a go, and sometimes I've wondered, while I've been sitting and scribbling away, how professional writers get along. I've tried to write, and then suddenly remembered I've left the soup on. The drains have become clogged up here at the cottage, and I've had to leave the writing and start flushing the loos. Do other writers do this? I don't know. Perhaps I'll stick to impersonations, though I must say, like so many things in my life, it's been fun.

Hang on – I've just seen Julie Walters on television. Now there's a good one to do . . . .